Portraits in Rhythm
Complete Study Guide
Observations and Interpretations of the
Fifty Snare Drum Etudes from Portraits in Rhythm

by Anthony J. Cirone

INTRODUCTION

The *Portraits in Rhythm Study Guide* contains a detailed analysis of the fifty snare drum Etudes from *Portraits in Rhythm*. These observations and interpretations represent many years of performing and teaching.

As with all music, there is no one interpretation; however, I hope these suggestions spark an interest in each student to develop a greater insight into a composer's musical intentions. As this text is studied and applied to each Etude, I expect these newly learned skills will carry over into other compositions and performances.

The first 25 Etudes originally appeared in Modern Drummer Magazine, and I wish to thank Ron Spagnardi for his cooperation in releasing them for publication. This publication contains an analysis of the entire 50 Etudes in one volume.

A.J.C.

TABLE OF CONTENTS

FOREWORD

What could be more challenging to a percussionist than extracting the greatest amount of music out of an instrument that supplies the least amount of possibilities? This challenge is presented to every concert snare drummer. The snare drum lacks most of the characteristics musicians look for when attempting to play musically. Basically, it has one sound and is very *staccato*—both undesirable elements when performing in a musical manner.

After considering these limitations, let's look at what is available to the performer:

1. Rhythm   2. Dynamics   3. Tempo   4. Phrasing   5. Interpretation

Although these musical elements are available to every instrumentalist, many of them are sacrificed for its single, most obvious element—rhythm. Musicians, however, can improve their performance by properly utilizing these elements as outlined below:

RHYTHM: I have a sign in my studio that reads: PRECISION, SENSITIVITY, MUSICALITY—three essential qualities for making music. Notice the first quality precision—this refers to rhythm. Without precise rhythm, the remaining qualities will not be effective. What good is a beautiful sound, even when played with sensitivity and musicality, if it is in the wrong place? I think we can all agree that our primary concern should be to place the notes in their correct position in the music.

Once we have properly placed the rhythms, our next concern should be focused on their accuracy. Rhythms should not be rushed, dragged, or interpreted in such a way as to be inconsistent with musical style or other performers.

Rhythm is very important and deserves our primary attention. When this element of music has been taken care of, then we can focus on other, equally important, areas of performance.

DYNAMICS: Dynamics add a great deal to music. They allow the more important solo lines to project while the accompaniment is heard at a softer level. They also add to the character of the music by creating many levels of sound within the work.

Performers are constantly involved with interpreting dynamics because they are not always played at the same level. Many factors enter into a decision on how loud a *forte* marking should be played; for example: (1). The size of the ensemble; (2). The size of the hall; (3). Whether a performance is indoors or outdoors; (4). Whether the stage has a shell or not; (5). The quality of the instruments being used; (6). Balancing the dynamic level with other performers; and, (7). Being flexible to the conductor's indications.

One simple decision a performer must make is deciding whether the dynamic marking is for an accompaniment or a solo part. If the entire orchestra has a *forte* marking, and the trumpet is the solo line, it is important for the other musicians to play slightly under the trumpet so the solo line projects.

One of the first lessons we learn as musicians is that dynamics are only relative. An obvious mistake by inexperienced musicians, when they are asked by the conductor to play louder or softer, is to utter the response, "But, my part says *forte* (or *piano).*" The conductor knows what the part says, he or she is just trying to adjust the balance.

TEMPO: Tempo is closely aligned to rhythm; however, it takes on another very important area of musicianship – the ability to follow the conductor. A performer may be playing accurately and with the correct dynamic, but if the conductor's tempo indications cannot be followed, a major problem will exist.

During the course of a performance, the conductor may make tempo changes (whether they have been rehearsed or not). It is the performer's responsibility to maintain eye contact with the conductor and to be flexible enough to adjust the tempo at any given time.

A musician may be a very gifted soloist and have tremendous command of the instrument, but if the player cannot follow the conductor, his or her value in the orchestra is limited.

Tempo is critical with regard to solo playing because it cannot vary haphazardly within the work. There is an enormous difference in adjusting tempo for musical reasons and just plain rushing or dragging.

PHRASING: Since much of the music written for percussion instruments is not phrased, the musical element of phrasing is a major consideration for percussionists. Phrasing is the composer's responsibility, but for many reasons, some composers do not feel the necessity of adding phrase markings to the percussion parts.

Whether these markings are present or not, music played by percussion instruments must be phrased in the same manner as any instrumentalist. When a percussion part does not have indicated markings, the performer must listen carefully to other instrumentalists to determine the proper phrasing.

Another concern is the ability to interpret phrase markings. Since the musical elements for snare drum are limited, the only method we have for phrasing is the use of accents, *staccato* marks, and dynamics. Although other instrumentalists phrase with longer or shorter sounds, this is not available to a snare drummer.

Two types of accents are available for phrasing. The first is the written accent which is played noticeably louder than an unaccented note. The second is the phrase accent, which is a subtler accent and should not be as loud as the written accent.

If a series of four sixteenth notes were written for snare drum and we wanted to phrase each group of four notes, a phrase accent or *staccato* mark should be placed on each of the first four notes. The remaining three notes would then be played softer than the first for the phrasing to be effective.

When performing music in mixed meters (for example, 3/8, 2/8, 3/8), the first note of each measure should have a phrase accent so meter changes can be felt. Since there is no standard marking for a phrase accent, I am using the *staccato* mark.

INTERPETATION: The final element is interpretation. This is the most difficult element to teach since a person's interpretation is basically his or her own opinion. As long as the elements of music are not compromised, an individual's own interpretation is valid for solo works.

A very important consideration in interpreting orchestral music is that it is the conductor's responsibility to instruct the performers on how to interpret the music. Performers must be flexible enough to interpret the music according to the conductor wishes.

It is also necessary for a soloist to create an interpretation of the music by analyzing its form and deciding what the composer originally intended. Then, using the elements previously discussed, construct a masterful performance.

ETUDE #1

After considering the information presented in the Foreword, I would now like to discuss the practical application of those music elements to a given composition. I have developed the following observations and interpretations throughout my years of performing and teaching; however, they do not preclude other interpretations. One of the greatest aspects of music is that no two performances are ever exactly alike. Listening to different recordings of classical symphonies by different conductors makes this evident. One factor, however, that should remain constant is the markings indicated by the composer in the score. The opening of Etude #1, for example, should begin with a loud dynamic and immediately *decrescendo* within two measures—how loud the performer begins and how much *decrescendo* is made is not always constant.

Another variable is tempo. Even though there are metronome markings for each Etude, every performer finds a comfortable tempo that may be faster or slower than indicated. Precision, sensitivity, and musicality, however, should not be sacrificed for speed.

Thematic material becomes obvious as these Etudes are studied. As I composed these pieces, I tried to write musically for the snare drum and included the same musical characteristics found in sonatas for violin, flute, etc. The idea of using rhythmic themes, therefore, became an important aspect when composing these etudes. The performer should be aware of thematic material and allow the themes to project.

OBSERVATIONS:

1. The opening measures present the rhythmic theme, which repeats in the second measure of line 6 and, again, in the last line. It should be heard as the beginning of a section each time this theme returns; therefore, the *ff* marking must be the loudest dynamic. The preceding accents should not be as loud as the statement of the theme.

2. The second measure of line 3 begins a series of three, two-measure phrases. Each two measures should be at a different dynamic level without a *decrescendo*.

3. All written accents should be noticeably louder than non-accented notes. The accents preceding each theme should also have a driving effect as they lead into the theme.

4. Use the center of the snare drum head for all loud playing and the edge of the head for all soft playing. When playing near the edge, the sticks should be over the snare bed.

INTERPRETATIONS:

1. The opening *decrescendo* should go from a *fortissimo* level to a *piano* level and then return to the *mezzo forte* at the third measure, increasing the effectiveness of the *decrescendo*.

2. The following *crescendo* into line 2 could be louder than a *fortissimo*; if it is, the *subito pp* will be more exciting. Remember, move quickly to the edge of the head for the *subito pp*.

3. The *pianissimo* in line 2 should not be softer than the triple *piano* in line 4.

4. There is no indication in line 8 explaining how soft to make the *diminuendo*. My interpretation is that it should decrease in sound until it can no longer be heard.

5. The series of loud and soft dynamics in line 10 should all be played in the center of the head. When a player moves too quickly between the center and edge of the head, the sound's quality changes very rapidly and the result is in poor taste.

1

Allegro assai ♩ = 132

ETUDE #2

The study of a piece of music for snare drum requires the same elements as for any orchestral instrument. As I discussed in the Foreword, musicians deal with rhythm, dynamics, tempo, phrasing, and interpretation. One element that does not apply is intonation. There is the consideration of properly tuning the snare drum, but I will not deal with it at this time.

Let's take a closer look at the area of interpretation. Because of the limited amount of information supplied by the composer, musicians must delve further into the music to determine a composer's intentions. I will be more specific with regards to Etude #2, but there are some general considerations that apply to all music.

Many pieces are composed with an idea in mind: a storm scene, a tranquil atmosphere, dancing, sadness, marching, etc. Music can express unlimited experiences; however, a great deal of music is not programmatic and will present a more difficult problem in developing the character.

Some elements that help us determine its character are:

1. Time Signatures:
This indication can change the character of the music. A marking of 4/4 is quite different from Cut Time. Also, writing in 3/8 time creates a different feeling from 3/4 time.

2. The Tempo Marking:
This is the one, most descriptive element a composer can provide to describe its musical character. If a composer indicates Moderato as the tempo marking, the only information we have is that the tempo is moderate; but, if the tempo marking says Moderato maestoso, we have much more information. This not only says the tempo is moderate, but that the notes must also have a majestic feeling.

3. The Rhythms:
The type of rhythms used can also help a player determine the work's character. Flowing triplets and non-syncopated rhythms are played differently from dotted notes and syncopated rhythms.

4. Accents:
The use of accents is a great help in adding to the work's character—even more helpful is the composer's use of normal accents, wedge accents, and *staccato* indications.

5. Rudiments (Flams, Drags, 4-Stroke Ruffs, etc.)
The use of these rudiments for snare drum parts creates a special character to the music. Other instrumentalists are able to create special inflections with their breath, fingers, embouchure, and bowing; percussionists create these inflections by controlling their sticks and using rudiments.

Each of the etudes in Portraits in Rhythm present different problems within the technical area of performance. Contending with all the dynamic and tempo changes throughout the book demands a certain level of technique. If a technical problem exists in studying one of the etudes, isolate the problem measures and create a technical exercise that incorporates the difficulty. For example, in Etude #2, the drags in line 11 are very difficult in a fast tempo. Pick out the two most difficult measures and repeat them, many times, until they can be played without stumbling.

Once the technical problems have been handled, turn to the more creative part of the study—its musical character. As with any musical work, if the character is not evident, then much of what the composer intends will be lost.

The tempo and phrasing have a lot to do with determining its character. Etude #2 has a metronome marking of 144 to the eighth note and a tempo indication of Allegretto; unfortunately, this does not tell the whole story. Allegretto means "quite lively and moderately fast." This, in itself, is an accurate description of the basic character, but it does not say too much about phrasing. The metronome marking may give us more information but, in this case, it is deceiving.

The indication is for the eighth note, indicating a pulse on each eighth note. A more accurate marking, however, would be for the dotted quarter note to equal 48, giving the impression of one pulse for each measure—a more accurate description of its character. The problem with an indication of mm = 48 for the dotted quarter note is the difficulty of practicing with such a slow pulse.

Beyond the two elements just discussed, the performer must determine actual phrasing. In a well-written piece of music, rhythms should also give some evidence of its character.

OBSERVATIONS:

1. To execute the *fp* markings in the third and fourth lines effectively, I suggest that one hand play the *forte* notes and the other hand play all of the remaining offbeats—with the exception of the thirty-second notes, which should be alternated.

2. As a general rule, all soft passages should be played near the edge of the head, and loud passages should be played near the center; however, when there are quickly changing dynamics, such as the *fp* in lines 3 and 4, they should be played in just one area of the head. When loud and soft dynamics change rapidly, in most cases, use the center of the head.

3. As discussed in #2, the *crescendo* and *decrescendo* markings in lines 7 and 8 should all be played in the center of the head.

4. The drags are to be played closed. This is generally true for all rudiments when playing in the Classical style.

3. The *sforzando* marking in line 6 indicates that the player should reinforce the dynamic above the current level. Since it comes in the middle of a *decrescendo*, in this case, it should not be very loud.

4. The sixteenth-note rolls in line 6 must be played using the 5-stroke roll because of the speed of this etude. This is the shortest roll possible—anything less would be executed as a drag. Use a closed orchestral roll and not an open rudimental roll.

5. The crush rolls in line 7 are played with both sticks simultaneously striking the drum.

6. Do not alternate flams or drags that follow in sequence (i.e., line 9). Play all of them either right-handed or left-handed; this will produce a more consistent sound.

INTERPRETATIONS:

1. This etude should be phrased with one beat per measure. A slight, natural accent is necessary on the first beat of every measure. A musical approach to phrasing the opening fourteen measures is as follows:

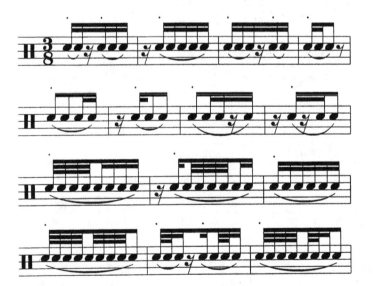

2. The thirty-second notes in lines 4 and 5 are to be alternated. Do not use double strokes for the thirty-second notes.

2

Allegretto ♪ = 144

ETUDE #3

In the previous Etude, I discussed the importance of character when learning a new composition. While preparing for a performance, examine the score for any hints the composer may give in order to discover his or her subtle ideas. These hints can be discovered by certain tempo, phrase markings, written directions, or explanations within the score.

Etude #3 is quite different from the first two studies, primarily because of its slower tempo, which dramatically changes the character. Snare drum music is rarely written in such a slow tempo because the obvious energy the snare drum produces is more compatible with fast-moving tempos and driving rhythms.

The key to this Etude's character is not so much the Moderato but the maestoso indication. A majestic feeling should be communicated within the opening measures by emphasizing each note. A more accurate notation would be to have a dash or *tenuto* mark on each note in the first two measures.

Although the tempo is marked mm = 69 to the quarter note, there are many measures with thirty-second notes. This gives the feeling of a rapid tempo and can change the character of the work. The secret of maintaining a Moderato maestoso feeling while playing rapid notes is never to lose the character of the quarter-note pulse. Although there may be a tendency to feel an eighth-note pulse during these measures, it should be avoided.

OBSERVATIONS:

1. Always be aware of the form in a given work. The dynamics clearly set off a series of three-measure phrases in the first three lines. The opening line can be described as a two-measure question with a one-measure answer. The second line is a one-measure question with a two-measure answer.

2. Remember in Etude #2, the *sforzando,* in line 2, means to reinforce the loudness at that point. It is not a *fp;* so, continue to play the first two triplets loudly so as to make the *decrescendo* more effective.

3. The compositional device used in the first two beats of measure nine is called augmentation. This is accomplished by taking the first beat of measure eight and playing it twice as slow. This results in a dramatic punctuation of the rhythm in measure nine as the piece begins a big *crescendo* into the next line.

4. To produce accented notes at a *fortissimo* level, increase the distance between the head and snare drum sticks. The greater the distance, the louder the sound. Do not force the sound by playing into the head.

5. The G.P. (Grand Pause or General Pause) at the end of line 7 indicates that no music is played in the measure. This sign is very helpful when performing orchestral music because all the players know it is a rest for everyone. Its use in a solo piece, such as this, is for musical emphasis. The performer should not move during this measure, but should hold the silence as though it were part of the piece. A Grand Pause measure is played in tempo—it is not a *fermata.*

6. Line 8 begins the recapitulation section where the original theme returns. A strong accent is needed for emphasis.

INTERPRETATIONS:

1. The 4-stroke ruffs in line 3 will sound more in the *maestoso* character if played on the open side.

2. The *diminuendo* in line 5 begins at *pianissimo* and disappears to nothing. Start the *pianissimo* at the edge of the head for a more delicate quality, as well as a softer sound.

3. All 5-stroke rolls are to be played closed. The accents on the ends of the rolls are important. The following *fp* must *crescendo* immediately; therefore, only the first stroke of the roll is played loud so the *crescendo* can start from a soft dynamic.

4. The *morendo* at the end of line 7 means "dying away." In studying a work, never pass by a word that is not understood. Look up its meaning in a dictionary to get a clearer understanding of the composer's intentions. The final measure should be slower and softer in order to play the *morendo* effectively.

3

ETUDE #4

Over the years, I have discovered certain Etudes work better for jury exams and recitals than others— Etude #4 is one of these. What makes this Etude more desirable for a solo performance is the musical elements within the piece. The more musical elements that are present, such as phrasing, dynamics, thematic material, and character, the more performers are able to express themselves during a performance.

This Etude has a tempo marking of Andante grandioso. Andante, referred to as a "walking tempo," indicates the tempo is not very fast, yet moves along at a comfortable pace. Now, we can understand why composers use Italian instead of English terms. I would have had to use five or six English words in order to describe one Italian term.

The *grandioso* gives us much more information regarding the character of the piece. Other words that describe *grandioso* are: magnificent, stately, dignified, and noble. It is the performer's job to create this character within the performance. Some elements in music that help us do this are: tempo, accents, phrasing, and dynamics. In addition to those markings indicated by the composer, we must add our own subtle elements to the degree necessary to create the character. This will be discussed further in the Interpretation section.

OBSERVATIONS:

1. The opening dynamic (in the first measure) requires a loud roll. A solid technique is important here. The roll should be of the same dynamic and character as the opening 4-stroke ruff and the following single strokes. The roll should not be pressed into the head or played too closed. The loud character is executed much better by using a more open roll; but, never to the extent of an open, rudimental, double-stroke roll.

2. All flams in line 2 should be played with the same hand. In other words, DO NOT ALTERNATE FLAMS. Use either all right-handed or left-handed flams to produce the same consistent sound throughout the line. Move slightly towards the center of the head for the *crescendo,* and back towards the edge for the *diminuendo.*

3. There are a number of instances in Portraits in Rhythm where long sections must be played very softly; for example, lines 7, 8, and 9 of this Etude. Probably the two most difficult techniques in snare drum playing are the loud rolls and very soft passages. Avoid any accents or phrase markings to execute these lines accurately. Choose a very sensitive area of the head, near the rim, to obtain a consistent sound and dynamic level throughout the three lines and keep the tips of the sticks close together.

4. Line 8 begins with a measure that includes a 4-stroke ruff, a drag, and a flam. This could be a stumbling block to the consistent articulation just discussed. I suggest creating an exercise out of this measure so it can be performed without unwanted accents or changes in the dynamic level.

5. The extreme dynamic changes in line 11 call for a triple *forte* with wedge accents (which are stronger than normal accents) and triple *piano,* which represents the softest dynamic. In this instance, I suggest playing in the center area of the head because both dynamics change so quickly. When dynamics change at such a rapid pace, the sound is more uniform when executed in only one area of the head.

INTERPRETATIONS:

1. The opening 4-stroke ruff gives the player an excellent opportunity to create a *grandioso* effect. An open 4-stroke ruff with a *crescendo* will sound more in character of the *grandioso* marking than a closed 4-stroke ruff. This is a matter of interpretation and, especially in solo playing, the player needs to use his or her imagination to create a truly musical expression.

2. To obtain a consistent sound in line 2, all flams should be played with the same hand. Never alternate long series of flams or drags in orchestral playing. The goal in maintaining a steady sound is better accomplished by using the same flam.

3. The second measure of line 4 begins a *forte* section; it easily lends itself to phrasing with two beats in the measure. A more accurate way of notating this is as follows:

A slight accent on the first and fourth beats of the measure, with a slight *diminuendo* over each half of the bar, will accomplish this.

4. I have found it a good practice to execute the offbeats in line 6 with one's weakest hand. Therefore, a right-handed person should play all the offbeat, sixteenth notes with the left hand.

5. The *crescendo* at the end of line 9 can be very exciting. The sound moves from the *pianissimo* passage to a *fortissimo*. I begin the *crescendo* slightly ahead of the marking in order to exaggerate the *crescendo* effect.

6. Most of the measured rolls in the book (such as the 5-stroke rolls in line 10) are to be played closed with an accent on the end on the roll.

4

ETUDE #5

Interpretation and character do not present as much of a problem in Etude #5. The problem here is basically rhythm and control. Many times, the simpler the rhythms and dynamics, the more trouble the work presents. Overcoming rhythm and control problems are no secret. Daily practice and continuous repetition of single, double, and closed-roll exercises are necessary in order to improve and maintain technique.

When students have a lack of technical ability, there will be problems with consistency and precision. Remember what I wrote in the Foreword, the sign in my studio says: "Precision, Sensitivity, Musicality"—three very important ingredients in making music. Carefully notice the first ingredient, Precision. Without precision in one's playing ability, there will be little sensitivity and musicality. What good does a beautiful sound or exquisite phrasing accomplish if the rhythms are rushed or imprecise? Precision comes from daily and repetitive practice of technical exercises. This repetition trains and strengthens the hands and wrists, giving them the ability to control rhythms and dynamics.

OBSERVATIONS:

1. The first 4 lines of Etude #5 have only one dynamic—*forte*. In order to execute single strokes, rolls, and rudiments (4-stroke ruffs, drags, and flams) at a constant *forte* dynamic, without unwanted accents, precision and control are necessary. The beginning and ending of rolls are of the most concern.

2. Line 6 begins with a series of three measures; each measure is softer than the preceding one. The challenge is to play each set of accents in the new dynamic.

3. The last measure of line 6 begins a very difficult section containing quarter-note triplets. This section determines the tempo of the work. The combination of quarter-note triplets with various other rhythms in the same measure makes this section particularly hard.

4. The final measure of the piece is a single eighth note at a *piano* level. Since it follows three very loud notes, play it in the center of the head. The dash above the note (*tenuto*) requires an emphasis in the dynamic level.

INTERPRETATIONS:

1. To obtain a full and consistent *forte* dynamic in the opening section, hold the rolls at that *forte* level. Do not press the rolls into the head—this will cause unwanted accents and a forced sound.

2. The 4-stroke ruffs in line 4 should be played close together (not too open). Avoid any accents on the end of the ruff, thereby maintaining the constant *forte* level mentioned earlier.

3. The accents in line 5 will be more effective if the unaccented notes are not played too loud. It is not necessary to overplay these measures even though the dynamic level is *fortissimo*. Always strive for musicality.

4. The difficult section, beginning in the last measure of line 6, can be practiced in the following manner: (a) Practice straight quarter-note triplets on the drum while tapping quarter notes with your foot; (b) Practice the passage in question without grace notes; (c) Practice the passage as written.

5

EL03626A

ETUDE #6

Snare drum music is quite often written at fast tempos. Other orchestral instruments such as the flute, clarinet, and violin can play long melodic lines in slow tempos with very expressive phrases. The snare drum however, with its *staccato* quality, can only extend its sound by using a roll.

Etude #6 incorporates some of the expressive qualities of other orchestral instruments into a solo with a quarter-note pulse of 63 and a tempo marking of Largo espressivo. The extensive use of dynamics, especially when rolling gives the player an opportunity to play expressively on the snare drum. Although the tempo is slow, this Etude utilizes rapid thirty-second notes in keeping with the natural character of the instrument. To obtain the proper effect of the tempo marking (Largo), retain the pulse of the quarter note. When learning this Etude, it is advisable to subdivide the beat into an eighth-note pulse for accuracy. Once the rhythms are learned, return to the quarter-note feeling.

Technique plays a big part in controlling dynamics. If the sticks are not held properly, unwanted accents will result and distort phrasing. If they are held too tightly, a *staccato* sound will result, also distorting the phrasing. Maintaining control over dynamics requires discipline in execution and a skilled technique.

OBSERVATIONS:

1. It is necessary to repeat the rule about moving between the center and edge of the head because of the many *crescendos* and *diminuendos*. **When moving quickly between loud and soft dynamics, stay in the center area of the head.** Use the edge of the head for soft sections. This not only gives the player a softer sound level, but also a more delicate quality. Use the center of the head for loud passages that require a full, deep sound. For example, in line 9, there is a series of thirty-second notes over the measure with the dynamics changing quickly from *fortissimo* to *piano*. Moving between the center and edge of the head will cause the quality of sound to change too quickly. Play this measure in the center area of the head.

2. Line 4 gives a perfect example of moving from the center of the head to the edge. The first measure of line 4 is played in the center, obtaining the full potential of the drum. The second measure needs a completely different character for the *pianissimo* thirty-second notes; therefore, move to the edge for these notes. It not only makes it easier to play softer, but also changes the quality to a more delicate sound.

3. The *fortissimo* roll, at the end of the first measure in line 6, is the loudest roll in the piece. This roll must take on an open character to be played properly; however, a roll with open double strokes (i.e., a rudimental roll) should not be used. Reducing the number of bounces within the stroke allows the roll to take on an open sound. A "buzz" or "press" roll may sound uneven when played at the *fortissimo* level.

4. Line 10 consists of two measures of triple *piano* thirty-second notes. This is the softest section of the Etude and can be very dramatic following the triple *forte* measure with wedge accents.

INTERPRETATIONS:

1. Although the *forte* in the first measure is under the last eighth note, the *crescendo* should peak on the downbeat of the second measure. Placement of dynamics by composers and copyists are frequently inaccurate. The performer must use judgement and make musical decisions in these cases.

2. The two rolls in measure three should both start at a *forte* level. The indication, as printed, might suggest that the second roll is softer; both rolls, however, should be identical.

3. Measure five reminds us of another important principle of orchestral snare drum playing: **Use one hand for single strokes in a series.** Whenever a part can be executed by one hand, it always produces a more even and consistent sound.

4. The two sixteenth-note rolls in line 3, measure one, are most effectively played as 5-stroke rolls. To use a longer roll might cause a forced sound and prevent the full, open sound needed here. Anything less than a 5-stroke roll would be in the drag or ruff category and incorrect.

5. Line 5, measure one, needs some clarification. The first *crescendo* does not indicate how loud one should play before the *diminuendo*. The first and second *crescendo* should be equal. A more accurate notation is as follows:

pp ——— *f* — *pp* <*f*> *pp*

6

ETUDE #7

I would like to say a few words about the proper placement and tuning of the snare drum. We have primarily been dealing with the music itself; yet, part of preparing for a recital or any solo performance is getting the best sound possible out of the instrument. The first decision is in choosing the proper drum. First, decide whether a gut (or cable) or wire snare drum is appropriate for a particular etude. Considering the etudes discussed so far, I suggest Etudes 1, 2, 6, and 7 be performed on a wire drum and Etudes 3, 4, and 5 on a gut snare drum. These decisions are based on the character, dynamics, and tempo of the piece. This is a personal decision and your judgement is just as valid.

I prefer performing on a drum with tight heads. This, again, is personal—each performer should feel comfortable with the tension placed on the heads.

The tension on the snares is also important. One common mistake is to tighten the snares so much that they choke the drum sound. I suggest tightening the snares only to the point of obtaining a crisp sound, without any rattles or buzzes, and no more.

Place the drum at a comfortable height, with a proper tilt (if any), and also place the strainer in a position where it can be easily reached.

Now, with the snare drum tuned properly and positioned correctly, we can deal with the music.

OBSERVATIONS:

1. I have always thought of this Etude as though it were written for two players. The first player would continually play the soft measures as an accompaniment, while the second player would perform the loud measures. The effect is that of a continuous rhythm (like measures three, four, and five) which underlies the entire work, interrupted only by the loud measures.

For one player to obtain this effect, a complete mastery of the dynamics and tempo is necessary. The difficulty is moving from loud to soft measures without changing tempo or distorting rhythm. Proper techniques for accomplishing this will be discussed in the Interpretation section.

2. Another approach in analyzing this Etude is to look at it as a series of "question-and-answer" phrases. The Etude begins with a series of two-measure "questions," followed by a three-measure "answer." As the work progresses, the number of measures in each phrase varies, but the effect remains the same.

3. The work is dynamically consistent, with a few exceptions: the *mezzo forte* in line 6 (which acts as a simple transition in the middle of the work); the *fortissimo* in line 7 which builds up to the climax; the triple *forte* in line 8 which is the climax; and the final statement at the end.

4. The most difficult part of the entire Etude is in line 9, measures two and three. The dynamics change very rapidly from the triple *forte* to the *piano* within a thirty-second note speed.

INTERPRETATIONS:

1. All of the loud sections should be phrased in one, with a slight accent on the first beat of each measure. The soft measures, however, should be as even as possible with no noticeable phrasing or accents.

2. The key to accurately and precisely performing this Etude is in executing all loud measures in the center of the head and all soft measures near the edge of the head. Remember, the effect is that of two players. By choosing a sensitive spot on the head (two or three inches from the edge), all of the soft passages will be consistent in sound. Always return to the center of the head so the loud sections will produce a full, deep drum sound.

The difficulty is moving from one area of the head to the other with precision. Any change in tempo or variation in dynamics will take away from the effect of the Etude. For instance, if a player delays the start of the soft measures while moving towards the edge of the head, the tempo will not be steady. If the player makes a slight *diminuendo* while changing from the loud to soft measures, the dramatic effect of the dynamic change will be lost.

3. I suggest all drags in a series (line 4, measure four) be played with the same hand. This helps to maintain a steady sound.

4. There is a slight problem with the notation during the roll measures in line 6. The first roll ends with a sixteenth note in measure seven, while the second roll is tied to another roll in measure eight. Performers need to pick up such inconsistencies in notation when studying a musical composition. In order to make these four measures sound similar, I suggest no articulation at the end of the first roll (downbeat of measure seven); instead, allow it to end with a roll sound. The final measure, however, of line 6 should begin with an articulated note so all four thirty-second notes are similar.

5. Please note the notation in line 7, measures three and four—they are rolls and not thirty-second notes. See Etude #46 for further clarification.

7

Allegretto ♪. = 88

ETUDE #8

In some of the earlier etudes, we discussed the need for phrasing in order to bring out certain groups of notes—this becomes even more important when dealing with studies in mixed meter. When a composer writes in a meter such as 7/8, the very nature of the division of the notes presents unequal patterns within the measure. The most common groupings are 4 and 3, or 3 and 4. It is also possible, however, to have groupings such as: 2,2,3 / 3,2,2 / 2,2,2,1 / 3,3,1, etc.

If a composer takes time to divide notes into definite groupings, the performer should make sure they are heard. If all the notes are performed equally, the listener would not be able to distinguish the mixed-meter phrasing. Remember, we are talking about solo works; when we play orchestral parts, this is not always true. Many times, snare drum parts are played evenly and without phrases. It is an interpretive decision and the conductor will usually have an opinion regarding such matters.

The phrases are executed by, what I refer to as, "natural accents." The first notes of each group must be articulated with a small accent so the phrasing can be brought out. These accents should not be so heavy so they are heard as written accents. It is more appropriate to place a dot or *staccato* marking on the first note of each phrase to insure the articulation. The remaining notes are then played softer and with a subtle *diminuendo*.

OBSERVATIONS:

1. On line 2, measures one, two, and four, there are slow quarter-note rhythms. One of the more common practices in orchestral snare drum playing, if the tempo permits, is to perform all similar note patterns with one hand. These measures are a good example. After the first two eighth notes in the first measure of line 2, play the remaining notes (until measure three) with one hand. Repeat this again in measure four.

2. One of the most common errors students make in sticking is to double a stroke in order to begin on their strong hand. For example, in line 4, measures three and four, there is a roll followed by three eighth notes and then an accented sixteenth pattern. A right-handed player will probably play the pick-up note to the roll with the left hand and begin the roll on the right hand. I agree with this because it is wise to lead with the strongest hand.

A normal execution for the following three eighth notes is to release the roll on the right hand and alternate the three notes. The eighth notes will, therefore, be played as R, L, R. When a player also wants to begin the accents with the strong hand, problems arise. Considering the previous sticking, the player will have to double the right hand in order to also begin the accents on the right hand. This may cause a slight distortion of rhythm and, many times, an unwanted accent because the last eighth note may be rushed and forced as it prepares for the next measure.

Solutions are as follows: (a) Release the roll on the left hand to prepare for the accents on the right hand. (b) Play the accents on the left hand. Players should not be so right or left-handed that they are unable to execute with either hand.

3. The triplet patterns in line 9 are followed by dotted sixteenth and thirty-second notes. When dotted notes and triplets are played together, be sure to play the thirty-second notes as short as possible so they do not sound like triplets.

INTERPRETATIONS:

1. As mentioned in the Introduction, groups of notes are to be phrased as written. Place a slight accent on the beginning of each group, allowing the phrases to be heard. A more accurate way of notating this passage is as follows:

2. Beginning at the second measure of line 8, there are groups of six, sixteenth notes over the three bars. The notes are connected over the barline in order to show the proper phrasing. This is a common practice in notation. This section could have also been written in 3/8 time. The same phrasing considerations in the beginning of the piece also apply here. The dynamics also help to shape this section.

8

Andante moderato ♪ = 192

ETUDE #9

We have discussed many technical and musical considerations during the first eight Etudes of Portraits in Rhythm. I would now like to begin delving into compositional considerations of a snare drum solo. As we approach the middle section of this book, I would like to point out certain devices used in creating these solos. By the time we get to Etude #23, which begins the section on musical form, I hope we will have enough information to clearly understand the compositional concepts.

This Etude presents a clear example of a snare drum solo with an opening theme that is repeated throughout the piece. Great Classical composers used this simple device (repetition) to create hours of magnificent music. The repetition of a theme is the key for organizing music in its simplest and most effective form. The factor that determines the success of this compositional device is variation. The way a composer handles a theme, as it continuously returns throughout the music, helps determine the work's success.

When writing for a melodic instrument, many ways are available for enhancing the variations: key changes, interval expansion or contraction, inversion, etc. They only work, however, when a melodic line is present. Snare drum music is concerned with one specific element – rhythm. This limits the use of such compositional devices, but there are still enough to maintain interesting variations. Some devices that apply to both melodic and rhythmic themes are: dynamics, tempo changes, articulation, and time signatures changes.

The opening four measures of Etude #9 expose the thematic material for this solo. It can easily be seen returning in lines 7 and 11. Each time the theme is presented, there is a variation in the music that follows. What sets this theme apart is the *decrescendo* and the *staccato*. Certainly, it is not the rhythm, which consists simply of eighth notes. As this solo is performed, each presentation of the theme should be clearly distinguished by the dynamic and *staccato* effect.

OBSERVATIONS:

1. The use of *staccato* in snare drum writing may seem a bit redundant, because the snare drum sound itself is very short and dry. What this marking does, however, is tell us that the sound should be exaggerated. I will discuss technical considerations later.

2. In line 2, measure four through seven, the *decrescendo* measures should be played as one phrase. Normally, when there are no phrase markings, a phrase is marked by bar lines. In this case, play the four measures as one phrase. A more correct notation is as follows:

3. Beginning at the last three bars of line 3, we have a series of three-measure phrases. The dynamics set this apart very clearly in a question-and-answer format. Following this are two, five-measure phrases.

4. Notice, there is a *forte* marking in the third measure of line 6, and another *forte* marking in the fourth measure of line 7, without any change in between. This may seem to be unnecessary; however, there is a good reason to repeat the *forte*. Since the theme returns in line 7, it is necessary to repeat the *forte* so the thematic material is exaggerated. The second *forte* actually takes on the character of an accent.

INTERPRETATIONS:

1. The *staccato* effect, in the opening, and when the theme returns, is produced by tightening the grip on the sticks by using more pressure at the fulcrum point where the sticks are held. The stick is also held more firmly in the hand by the remaining fingers. This technique is only used when a tight, dry sound is needed, The amount of tension will determine the level of *staccato* sound.

2. In line 7, the last three measures begin a series of dotted sixteenth and thirty-second notes. Be sure the thirty-seconds are on the short side, especially when the triplets begin in the next line. The danger here is in playing the thirty-second notes like a triplet.

3. All of the grace notes (4-stroke ruffs, drags, flams and 7-stroke rolls) are to be played closed, as in orchestral style.

4. The 7-stroke roll is especially difficult to execute because the tempo is very fast. The solution is to begin the roll very close to the first beat of the measure.

EL03626A

ETUDE #10

The natural feeling of 9/8 time creates three groups of three beats to a measure. This grouping is used throughout the Etude. This natural pulse is only disturbed at the end by the use of accents. Always be aware of the natural phrasing, and place appropriate emphasis on the beginning of each group.

The opening four measures set the tone for the entire Etude. Because the rhythms are simple and uncomplicated, exaggerate the phrasing. When later rhythms are affected by ornamentation and dynamics, other emphasis will be necessary.

Etude #10 deals more with the technical aspects of drumming rather than compositional aspects. The opening theme is never exactly repeated; however, these measures represent one of the two thematic elements. The second important consideration, thematically, are the measures of dotted sixteenth and thirty-second notes. This Etude consists of two rhythmical ideas, developed by using of dynamics, ornamentation, and accents.

OBSERVATIONS:

1. As just discussed, phrasing should be three beats per measure. Accomplished this by placing a natural accent (slight) on the first note of each group.

2. Remember, one of the basic rules of orchestral drumming is to play consecutive flams with the same hand, as in line 2, measure one.

3. Whenever dotted rhythms are used, such as in line 3, the shorter notes (in this case, the thirty-second notes), should always be played on the quick side. Let this rhythm come alive by keeping the thirty-second note short and by moving forward.

4. Line 3 begins a series of dynamic levels and each level should be considered a plateau unto itself. Be careful not to *crescendo* into the next measure. The dynamic change should be immediate and dramatic. The difficulty here is that the change must come within the space of a thirty-second-note rhythm. Begin the *pianissimo* near the edge of the head; then, as the dynamics increase, quickly move closer to the center of the head.

5. When the dotted thirty-second notes are combined with triplets in line 11, exaggerate the quickness of the thirty-second notes even more. The danger here is if the thirty-second notes are relaxed, they may sound like a triplet rhythm—a common mistake for students.

INTERPRETATIONS:

1. In line 7, the first measure contains a drag, flam, 5-stroke roll, and a 7-stroke roll. These rudiments are to be played closed—as in the orchestral style. Start the 7-stroke roll very close to the rest to properly fit it in at the indicated tempo. If the tempo is slower, the roll can be delayed a bit more.

2. The rolls in line 8 should be played on the open side; that is, do not crush the sound by trying to play loudly with a roll that is too closed. It is also important to release the roll with a solid, single stroke so all the notes of the following rhythms can be clearly heard.

3. I suggest the following sticking pattern (flam taps) for the flams and strokes in line 9:

It is also possible to alternate as follows:

4. Line 10 begins a series of accents with thirty-second-note rhythms. My suggestion is to alternate the sticking throughout this section. One mistake students sometimes may make is to double the thirty-second notes. This is not only more difficult to execute, but usually results in uneven rhythms and unwanted accents.

5. The final consideration is the wedge accents in the last measure. They indicate a stronger attack than normal accents; so, be sure to reserve the loudest sounds for the final four notes.

10

Moderato ♩. = 69

ETUDE #11

There are certain etudes that seem to work especially well for solo recitals or jury exams—Etude #11 is one of these. The fact that it is so thematic and the rhythms move quickly, with many dynamic changes, gives the performer a chance to show off his or her technique and musical ability.

The opening theme in measures one through four is never actually repeated; however, it does return in lines 7 and 10 with some variation. Each time the theme returns, emphasize the opening rhythm as a climatic point of the work. This exaggeration helps the listener to focus on the form, and it also adds an element of cohesiveness to the performance.

OBSERVATIONS:

1. The metronome marking is listed as eighth note = 132. This gives a clue as to the phrase emphasis. When the eighth note is listed as the primary pulse, be sure to exaggerate each eighth-note pulse and not the dotted quarter-note pulse.

2. Line 3 begins a series of rhythms at a *piano* dynamic. The ability to play rapid rhythms at a soft dynamic without unwanted accents or changes in dynamics is one of the most difficult snare drum techniques to perfect. Choose a spot near the edge of the head in order to obtain a delicate quality for this section.

3. The measure that takes up the entire fifth line, again pairs up two very contrasting rhythms of dotted notes and triplets. In this case, it is a dotted thirty-second and sixty-fourth note against a thirty-second-note triplet. As is usually the case when performing these rhythms, make the sixty-fourth note as short as possible to avoid any resemblance of a triplet feeling.

4. Line 8, measure one, employs what is called "augmentation." This is a compositional device that repeats a rhythm twice as slow as previously heard. In this Etude, the first two beats of line 8 directly quotes the third and fourth beats of line 7.

5. The first measure of line 9 presents a very interesting situation where the performer must articulate a very soft, closed roll and single strokes. Moving between these two techniques can be quite challenging. The execution must have no distortions in either the rhythm of the thirty-second note rhythms or the beginning of the roll.

INTERPRETATIONS:

1. Treat the opening three notes of the theme (measure one) equally and with some emphasis (accents). The remainder of the measure may be phrased on the eighth-note pulse. A more accurate notation for this interpretation is as follows:

2. Notice the accented notes at a *forte* level in line 5. The danger here is to underplay the <u>unaccented</u> notes. There must be a contrast between the unaccented *forte* notes and the following *piano* marking.

3. When the theme returns in lines 7 and 10, a roll is added. Do not tie the roll into the sixteenth note. By separating the roll from the note, the sixteenth note will be heard as a distinct note and not part of the roll. This keeps the character of the theme consistent with the opening measure.

4. I have indicated a possible sticking for the last half of line 7. This sticking is for a right-handed player and can be reversed for a left-handed percussionist. I use a double stroke so I can return to my strong hand for the accents. This way, both sets of accents are played identically and, hopefully, equally.

5. Line 11 has a series of thirty-second notes with a *diminuendo* and *crescendo*. Part of the interpretative process is to determine how much dynamic change is appropriate during this measure. My personal feeling for solo works such as this is to exaggerate both levels of dynamic changes in order to add as much interest as possible to the music.

6. The final line has a series of quickly changing dynamics. Play the loud dynamics in the center of the head and move closer to the edge for the softer notes.

11

Adagio ma con spirito ♪ = 132

ETUDE #12

Etude #12 focuses on two important elements of music—mixed meter and superimposed rhythms. Mixed meters occur when moving from one time signature to another with different pulse values; that is, when the lower number of the time signature changes. In this case, the change is from 2/4 to 3/8.

Mastering this change requires two simple rules: (a). Count the proper number of beats in each measure. (In 2/4, count two beats to the measure and in 3/8, count three beats to the measure.) (b). Tap your foot on each quarter-note pulse in the 2/4 measures and for the dotted quarter-note pulse in the 3/8 measures.

The correct counting procedure for the eighth-note pattern in a 2/4 and 3/8 combination is as follows:

The combination of rhythms used in Etude #12 is a bit more complicated—counting procedures will be explained later.

The second important element (superimposed rhythms) is the quarter-note triplets. The ability to play these rhythms correctly depends on the player's skill in performing three beats against two beats. Practice by playing three beats with the right hand and two beats with the left hand. The counting is as follows:

Now, switch rhythms; three beats with the left hand and two with the right. When performing this rhythm within the context of the music, the foot beats twice while the sticks beat the triplet. Now, try the above rhythm with the foot and hands.

OBSERVATIONS:

1. The first example of the quarter-note triplet in measure three divides the second note into a dotted eighth and sixteenth rhythm. Count the sixteenth notes with the vowel a; the measure is then counted: 1 2 a 3.

2. If the first rule above is applied to the last three measures of line 1, the proper counting will be as follows:

3. The end of line 3 presents a very difficult transition (where the quarter-note triplet is followed by a 3/8 measure). The key to properly performing these measures is to have a strong quarter-note pulse with the foot so the eighth-note pulse in the 3/8 measure is against the 2/4 pulse and not the quarter-note triplet pulse.

4. A similar transition occurs in line 6 where the 3/8 is followed by a 2/4 measure with quarter-note triplets. First, practice this transition using only your foot. Concentrate on the foot playing the dotted quarter-note pulse in the 3/8 and straight quarter notes in the 2/4. Now, as you are concentrating on the foot pattern, play the snare drum rhythms as written.

5. In line 7, where the 2/4 and 3/8 measures alternate at the *fortissimo*, count in the following manner:

INTERPRETATIONS:

1. When composers write in mixed meters, their intention is usually to create a sense of shifting patterns. The key to proper interpretation is in phrasing. Take, for example, the last two measures of line 1. Here, we have a 2/4 and 3/8 pattern with steady sixteenth notes. If a player chooses to play these notes evenly, there will not be any feeling of shifting patterns. I believe, to accurately present the composer's desires, a player must phrase each group of sixteenth notes so as to create the proper feeling of a mixed meter—a slight accent at the beginning of each group of notes will accomplish this.

2. Notice the plateau of dynamics in line 3. The first measure of quarter-note triplets is *fortissimo*, with each succeeding measure marked noticeably softer. Begin in the center of the head for the *fortissimo* and move closer to the edge for each dynamic change. Remember, all flams should be played with the same hand for consistency of sound and character.

3. Line 5 is another good example for phrasing each group of notes so as to create a strong mixed-meter feeling.

12

Andante con animato ♩ = 84

1.

2.

3.

4.

5.

6.

7.

8.

9.

10.

EL03626A

ETUDE #13

Etude #13 provides us with the most musically complete snare drum solo so far. This short work contains an Introduction, an Exposition section, a Trio, and a Coda. As snare drum players, we rarely find ourselves concerned with such musical components in most of the literature we perform. The musical considerations presented in this solo, however, are actually very common to most instrumentalists.

As percussionists, we tend to focus on rhythm and dynamics because they compromise 90% of the music we perform. Once a student progresses from an amateur to a professional, there are, however, other elements of music equally as important. This solo, for instance, will consider: *fermatas,* a *cesura* (pause), *ritard,* seven tempo changes, and some Italian words used to describe a certain character.

The importance of dealing with these musical considerations is not only to have the knowledge of their meaning, but, also, to develop a certain amount of technique in order to execute them properly. As a student contends with changes in tempo, dynamics, phrasing, character, etc., the degree of success will be related to the student's technical, as well as, mental abilities.

Personally, I do not even attempt to have students study from Portraits in Rhythm until they have successfully developed their technical and reading abilities. If I am constantly dealing with incorrect hand positions, or use of the wrist and arms, or must correct reading errors, or missed dynamics, there is very little time left to discuss the musical considerations of the piece.

Now, with this as a background, let us observe and interpret the many musical considerations of Etude #13.

OBSERVATIONS:

1. The opening tempo marking is Maestoso, which we may remember means "majestically." The metronome marking is quarter note equals 52; so, already we know the opening will be slow and very dramatic. An introduction does exactly that—it introduces something. It sets the character of the work and should immediately get the attention of the audience. In this case, a very slow Introduction leads to a fast Exposition.

2. The Allegro con brio, at 144 to the quarter note, is a very typical snare drum part and tempo. Be aware of the wedge accents in the first measure of line 3; they are played more dramatically than normal accents. Also, remember to move the sticks to the edge of the head for the *piano* section in line 4, and then back to the center during the *crescendo* in measure one, line 5.

3. The Exposition ends right before the Waltz section with a *ritard* and a *diminuendo*. Musical elements, such as these, have a way of separating sections of music so the listener can be prepared for the new tempo. They also allow the performer to display a great amount of musical sensitivity. Skimming over these elements does a great disservice to the composer; use them to create moments of excitement and subtlety.

4. The Largo section also uses the Italian words, *e molto pesante.* The performer must translate these words in order to properly play the passage. Never skip over words you do not understand, whether they are in English or Italian. Everything the composer puts on the page has some meaning and will add clarity to the composer's original intention. I will discuss how I interpret this in the next section.

5. The following Allegro con brio begins the Coda. This, of course, is the same music as the Exposition so try to retain the identical tempo. A Coda usually contains music we have already heard before.

INTERPRETATIONS:

1. Notice carefully where the *fermata* is located in the first two measures. The *fermata* is placed on the quarter note and not on the roll itself; this makes a difference in interpreting the measure. If the *fermata* were on the roll, then the roll would be held at the player's discretion. Since the *fermata* is on the quarter note, however, it indicates that there will be some silence between the quarter note and the next measure. The entire Introduction should not have a sense of tempo; it should have the effect of a fanfare—each measure a separate entity.

2. The two slashes at the end of the first line (*cesura* or commonly called railroad tracks) are a sign indicating the music should come to a stop. The length of the pause is an interpretive decision and left up to the performer—usually, it is short.

3. The measure before the Waltz section presents a great musical opportunity. All the elements in this measure, *ritard, diminuendo,* and the *fermata,* combine, allowing the performer to "shine." Some decisions that make this measure more effective are: how much to slow down; when to begin slowing down; when to get softer; how long to hold the *fermata;* and how soft to play. Even though the markings are placed under certain notes, they can be interpreted, making the music more effective.

4. The Waltz tempo begins with a traditional snare drum accompaniment. I suggest the opening four measures be played with one hand and, in order to add more character, play it in the style of a Viennese Waltz. This is where the second beat is actually played early.

5. When the Waltz theme begins after the repeat sign, exaggerate the second beat of the first measure by placing a *crescendo* on the preceding roll and lifting the stick off the drum as the second beat is played. This happens again in the fifth measure of the theme.

6. Now, we come to the Largo section where the words *e molto pesante* are added. If you have looked up these words in an Italian dictionary, you now know they mean "and very heavy." I suggest exaggerating this music by placing a heavy emphasis on each note. The composer can also get this effect with the use of accents or *tenuto* marks; but the word "heavy" brings a certain connotation with it, creating a greater feeling in the music.

7. Notice the *fermata* on the final note of line 9. After holding the roll, immediately begin the Allegro con brio. There is no rest or silence between the Largo and the Allegro.

13

ETUDE #14

As we have progressed through the etudes of Portraits in Rhythm, it should become evident that, in addition to technical considerations, musical form and phrasing are two areas of continuous concern. I stress this because most snare drummers are not adequately trained in this area. Also, many of the phrase markings are not included in the music.

Etude #14 is a straightforward example of music in 3/8 time with a slight inclusion of 2/8 in the middle of the work. The standard approach to phrasing 3/8 time is to place an emphasis on the first beat of each measure. It is also possible, however, that the first theme (the first seven measures) could be played as one long phrase or broken up into several phrases. The next three examples show the possibilities of phrasing these measures. When the phrase marks are omitted in a solo work, such as this, a performer must decide on the interpretation. Each phrase is articulated with a slight accent.

The musical form of Etude #14 begins with a statement of the theme, and is followed by a short transition in line 3 to a second theme (line 3, measure six). A simple development of the opening music follows, and then returns to the original theme with ornamentation (line 7, measure three). Finally, there is a statement of the theme at the end. By realizing its musical form, a return of the themes can be stressed; thereby, presenting a more educated performance.

OBSERVATIONS:

1. The opening theme is immediately repeated with accents, determining where the phrase emphasis is placed. In this case, the accents are in contrast to the normal 3/8 phrasing, so the second statement will sound quite different. Remember, an accent is played much stronger than a phrase marking.

2. The second theme begins in line 3, measure six, with a series of very soft rolls. The two most difficult technical areas of snare drum playing are very soft and very loud rolls. Be sure the rolls are not pressed into the head. Soft rolls do not need much pressure or speed. The secret is to produce a simple, sustained sound by gently playing a multiple bounce stroke on each stick without accents.

Remember, these two important considerations when playing a soft roll: (a). Do not to put too many bounces in each stroke because the result will be an uneven roll, and (b). do not try to play it too rapidly, because it will sound too loud.

3. In line 6, measure five, there are a series of eighth-note rolls tied to an eighth note with an accent. At the indicated tempo marking (mm = 96), a closed 5-stroke roll will work best. The first three rolls are in 3/8 time; the next three, in 2/8 time, and three more in 3/8 time. The rolls should "feel" differently because of the time signature change (3/8 to 2/8 to 3/8). In 3/8 , the rolls will "feel" syncopated; in 2/8, they will not. It will be evident if you tap your foot on the first beat of each measure as indicated below:

4. The original theme returns in line 7, measure three, with the addition of flams and drags. Experience has shown me the most effective way to stick passages, such as this, is to alternate strokes. A left stroke, therefore, is followed by a right flam or drag, and a right flam or drag is followed by a left stroke. The sticking I prefer is as follows:

5. One final observation: Because the original theme is repeated exactly in the final seven measures, be sure its phrasing is the same as the opening.

INTERPRETATIONS:

1. The last measure of line 2 begins a series of rudiments, including, a 7-stroke roll, a 5-stroke roll, a 4-stroke ruff, a drag, and a flam. The manner is which these rudiments are performed depends on the context of the work. As a general rule, rudiments are played closed in the Classical style. When the music has a military feeling, play the rudiments in an open manner. Since this is a solo work and the 3/8 time signature does not suggest a military character, perform the rudiments in a closed manner.

2. In line 4, measure four, there are six measures of untied rolls. In most snare drum literature, we cannot depend on the composer to use a tie when connecting a roll to the following note. Normally, the roll should be tied to single notes even when the tie is left out. In orchestral music, a determination is made by listening to other instrumentalists, and then, by matching their phrasing. I have been very careful to use a tie when appropriate in Portraits in Rhythm, so, if a roll is untied, it should be played as such. The last two measures of line 4 have a roll followed by a drag. Regardless of the notation, a roll cannot be tied into a flam or drag.

3. As mentioned before, the rolls in line 5 are to be 5-stroke rolls. This, of course, would only be accurate at the given tempo marking. If the tempo were slower, a longer roll would be needed, such as a 7- or 9-stroke roll. This brings up the subject of teaching measured rolls. I do not believe measured rolls should be taught immediately to beginning students. It gives them a deceptive understanding of the nature of a roll (which is a sustained sound). Measured rolls work best in a March tempo and I find it beneficial to introduce them after teaching the long roll. (For more information, see The Orchestral Snare Drummer by A.J. Cirone, Published by Warner Bros. Publishing Co.)

4. The last two measures of line 5 would be more accurately notated with a phrase marking over the two measures (also suggested by the *diminuendo*). Be sure the dotted quarter note is not accented—it ends the phrase.

5. It is important to remember the rule for playing flams or drags in series in orchestral music—**Do not alternate flams or drags in a series.** In line 8, there are a series of drags from measure two until measure five. Play them all in the same manner; that is, either all right-handed or left-handed. This should be determined by whatever drag was used in measure two—the first in the series of repeated drags.

14

ETUDE #15

Snare drum rhythms in 6/8 time are usually associated with marches. Marching music generally has an emphasis in either a duple or triple feeling. It is clearer to write the triple feeling in 6/8 time than to use triplets in 2/4 time. Etude #15, however, has very little to do with marching music. The opening measures suggest a rhythm that is actually very uncharacteristic of normal 6/8 music. The rhythms of this Etude are syncopated and produce a contemporary-sounding exercise. Another interesting feature of this Etude is that it uses three types of snare drum rolls: tied, untied, and crush rolls. I will say more about this later.

Very little phrasing is possible in the first two measures because of the nature of the rhythms. In normal 6/8 time, each measure is played by phrasing every three beats, however, because of the tied notes, this effectively removes the possibility of a consistent phrasing pattern. I suggest both measures be played as equal notes.

Musical elements (such as accents, flams, drags, crush rolls, tied notes, dynamics, etc.) all affect the performance of phrases. Each of these rudiments alters the phrasing by determining where the emphasis will be placed in the measure.

OBSERVATIONS:

1. The opening theme should be played as equal notes—avoid the tendency to rush. It is crucial to accurately place the second note in measure two. Since the last eighth note in measure one is tied to another dotted eighth note, there is quite a bit of silence—this may produce a tendency to rush.

2. In measure three, the roll is followed by a drag. Remember, a roll cannot be tied into a flam, drag, or 4-stroke ruff. There must be a break after the roll in order to set up for the drag. Some composers inadvertently tie rolls into these rudiments; this, however, is not practical. Do not end the roll with a single stroke because it adds another rhythm to the measure. Think of adding a rest just before the drag.

Incorrect

Correct

3. The last two measures in line 3 are untied rolls. When analyzing snare drum music, it is not always clear whether a composer actually intends the rolls to be untied or if it is simply an omission in notation. In most Classical orchestral literature, the player cannot depend on the notation of tied and untied rolls. In many cases, composers will not tie rolls to the following note, (or even to another roll). In most musical situations, however, it is necessary to tie rolls together and also into single notes.

Although this problem still exists in contemporary snare drum writing, it is to a much lesser degree. In method books such as Portraits in Rhythm, composers usually indicate their preference and these indications should followed carefully. Since the rolls are not tied into the sixteenth notes at the end of line 3, the note after the roll is more exaggerated—and this is the intention. When a roll is separated from the note, the note becomes connected to the following music.

4. Line 4 begins with a series of single notes and crush rolls. The normal notation for a crush roll is a dot above the roll. All rolls that must be played quickly, and are not tied, should be played as crush rolls. The crush roll is executed by simultaneously pressing both sticks on the head; this produces a very short sounding roll and it can be played quickly. A crush roll has no definite length; therefore, the note value does not matter. In effect, a dot over a quarter note or an eighth note will be played as the same crush roll in a fast tempo.

INTERPRETATIONS:

1. The last measure of line 1 has a short *crescendo* and *decrescendo* roll. To effectively transform the first roll from *piano* to *fortissimo* within a short span of time, open up the roll as it gets louder. Start the roll with closed, multiple bounces, and quickly broaden the strokes into an open roll. The *crescendo* is easier to produce with an open roll. Conversely, for the second roll (*fortissimo* to *piano*), start it as an open roll and increase the number of bounces in each stroke as it becomes softer.

2. The third line begins a series of dotted sixteenth notes. All the notes in the first two measures are the same length. Play all the notes with one hand. Remember, in orchestral snare drum writing, sound and control are of primary importance. The use of one hand for similar notes or patterns allows the player a great deal of control and helps to produce a consistent sound.

3. The *diminuendo,* going into line 7, ends with a dynamic of four *pianos.* The passage begins at two *pianos,* telling the performer that the end of the *diminuendo* must be as soft as possible—almost imperceptible.

15

ETUDE #16

The first two measures of Etude #16 are directly quoted from Ravel's famous orchestral composition, Bolero. Percussionists recognize this work as one of the most celebrated snare drum excerpts in orchestral literature. A musician may not feel challenged by the rhythm at first glance; in fact, the opening two measures do not present any particular rhythmical problems. The challenge comes from other considerations:

1. It begins as a solo for the snare drum.
2. The rhythm must be maintained at an extremely soft dynamic.
3. The orchestra is dependent on the rhythm's consistent accuracy.
4. The player's concentration is essential so as not to reverse the measures.

It is not uncommon for the player to become nervous because of these demands. If this happens, it will be difficult to control the sticks and execute the opening measures at such a soft dynamic.

Players have devised a number of "tricks" to overcome the problem of playing at such a soft dynamic. Some begin the work by playing with two quarters on the head. I have even seen a player start the piece by holding the sticks down at the tip; then, slowly creeping back (as the dynamics get louder) to the normal position. In the final analysis, there really are no shortcuts—it takes technique and control to master snare drumming. The following suggestions may be of help to students performing the snare drum part to Bolero.

The first concern is sticking. A normal sticking pattern for Bolero might be as follows:

A basic hand-to-hand alternate sticking pattern works best for most snare drum parts. When under such extreme pressure, however, as playing this rhythm on stage in front of 3000 people, with your colleagues looking at you, a cold sweat may develop, the knees may begin to weaken and, quite possibly, the brain may seem to stop functioning! If one (or all) of these symptoms develop, the first sign of trouble will be felt in the weaker hand. A right-handed player begins to lose control of the left hand and vice versa. I recommend the following sticking to counter this for a right-handed player (reverse for left-handed players):

This sticking will place most of the control on the right hand; therefore, the left hand has a less demanding role. As the dynamic increases, the sticking can be changed to the normal alternating pattern.

Controlling "nerves" is another matter. Today, many orchestras offer clinics on stress. We are all uniquely individual and react differently to the pressures of performing. The following are a few suggestions that might help when preparing for parts such as Ravel's Bolero.

1. Warm-up well in advance of the concert to be technically prepared to perform.
2. Take a few moments before going on stage and quietly think through what is about to take place. Play the part in your mind.
3. If possible, practice the part on stage—by yourself—before the first orchestral rehearsal.

OBSERVATIONS:

1. Although this Etude is fashioned after the famous snare drum part in Ravel's Bolero, each repetition of the solo measures is presented in different metric settings, which alters the phrasing.

2. As with the original part, the dynamic begins at *pppp* (that is, as soft as possible) and continues to increase in volume until the final note. The continuous *crescendo* should always be present. Each succeeding measure must be slightly louder than the previous one—creating an exciting climax. In the actual solo, the player must keep the snare drum part at *pppp* for quite a while before beginning the *crescendo*.

INTERPRETATIONS:

1. Place a natural accent on the first note of every group of notes in order to properly phrase each measure. Tapping the foot along with the natural accent is also helpful.

2. One exception to tapping the foot at the beginning of each group of notes occurs in the 5/16 excerpt in line 6. I suggest tapping the foot on the downbeat of each measure for this variation because the notes are tied over the barline. This means the foot will come between the triplet in the third measure of line 7.

3. The natural accents (and the foot) occur on each eighth note in the 2/16 variation in line 8.

16

Tempo di Bolero ♩ = 76

ETUDE #17

To some students, rhythms with constant mixed-meter changes, such as Etude #17, can be a nightmare. Most of our early training is with 2/4, 3/4, and 4/4 time. When something other than these standard meters is presented, it looks very difficult. I have always been in favor of teaching mixed meters to very young students. What students learn when they are young will always stay with them.

Without early training in mixed meters, music such as Etude #17 may look unplayable; when, in fact, it should be no more of a challenge than 2/4 time. I encourage all students, especially those not previously familiar with mixed-meter time signatures, to make a thorough study of this Etude. The following are a few basic rules for counting mixed-meter time signatures:

1. The bottom number of the time signature determines which note value will be counted as the main beat; for example, in 4/4 time, it will be the quarter note and in 3/8 time, the eighth note. In this Etude, which is in 3/16 time, it will be the sixteenth note.

2. Always count the proper number of beats as determined by the top number of the time signature. In 3/16 time there will be three counts, in 5/16 time, five counts, etc.

3. For example, in 2/4 time, the counting is as follows:

In 3/8 time, we use the same relationship; that is, the eighth note receives the main count, the sixteenth note is counted as eighth notes, and the thirty-second notes are counted as sixteenths.

In 3/16 time, the sixteenth note receives the main count, the thirty-second note is counted as an eighth, and the sixty-fourth note is counted as a sixteenth.

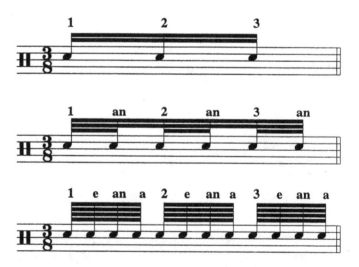

Etude #17 uses only time signatures in sixteenth time—that is, 2/16, 3/16, and 5/16. The relationship, therefore, in counting the rhythms will be constant. The sixteenth note gets the main count, and the thirty-second notes are counted with the use of "an". Also, remember that an eighth note gets two counts and a dotted eighth note gets three counts. I hope, by following these rules, the mystery of mixed meters will be simplified and no longer seem unusual. This subject is covered in more detail in Etude #47.

OBSERVATIONS:

1. The symbol sixteenth note = sixteenth note between measures three and four in line 1, tells us that the speed of the sixteenth note in the 3/16 measure is the same as the speed of the sixteenth note in the 2/16 measure. When the note values are equal (as these are), the relationship between the note values are the same. In future etudes, we will deal with mixed meters with differing values.

2. In line 8, notice the roll is not tied into the last measure of this line. Since the last measure begins with a flam, the roll must be separated so both hands can play it.

3. Beginning with the second measure of line 10, we find a series of thirty-second notes. Notice the accents are not always lined up with the division of the notes. In the 5/16 measure, for instance, the notes are divided into groups of 3 and 2; the accent, however, comes in the middle of the group of three which results in a feeling of 2 and 3. This creates a syncopated effect against the 3 and 2 division. If the performer beats his or her foot on the accents, the syncopated feeling will be lost. I suggest the following pattern for tapping the foot so the proper syncopation can be felt:

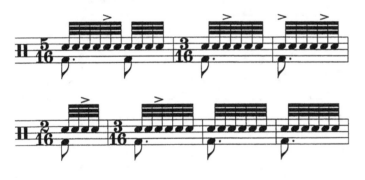

INTERPRETATIONS:

1. The first four measures make up one phrase, which is then immediately repeated. The natural accents should fall on the first note of measures one and five. To exaggerate this phrase, add a subtle *diminuendo* over each four measures. The following is a more accurate way to notate this:

2. At the end of line 3, there are a series of short rolls with a dot over each one. This normally denotes a crush roll; these, however, are all long rolls. They may look like crush rolls because they are written in 3/16 and 2/16 time, but, in this case, my intention is that the performer place a subtle accent on each roll; thereby, providing a fresh attack.

3. Following these rolls in line 4 is a series of thirty-second note rhythms that should be played near the edge of the head and phrased according to groupings.

4. There is not one way to "stick" any given passage. I do, however, like to follow certain rules when performing orchestral music. I would, for instance, suggest the following sticking for a right-handed player beginning with the last measure of line 8. This sticking follows the basic rules of alternating into flams and leading with the strong hand.

5. The final measure has a *fermata* over the rest on the first beat. The *fermata* is strictly for dramatic purposes, and its length is left up to the performer. This accomplishes a moment of silence before the final roll. If the *fermata* is too short, the roll will not stand out. If the *fermata* is too long, the dramatic effect will be lost.

44

17

ETUDE #18

I'd like to begin this page with some general philosophical thoughts regarding Portraits in Rhythm and why I believe it has become so popular. "Things" – books included – catch on because they fill a need and offer something unique to a very demanding and scrutinizing public. I've concluded that Portraits in Rhythm has done so well because players have been able to identify with the etudes' musical form. It's not that any one of the etudes is in any particular form; rather, they follow some principle of musical form that allows both musician and listener to relate to the ideas presented in a logical and practical manner. When considering the popularity of Western European music and its endurance over the centuries, we notice a very strong element of musical form. I've based my etudes on similar principles, and believe this same success has applied to Portraits in Rhythm.

With this background information in mind, I would now like to discuss Etude #18. I chose the foregoing analysis for this work because I borrowed the idea from Offenbach's light opera, "Orpheus and the Underworld"—the borrowed section is from the "Can Can", a popular dance of the late 19th century. The Etude is not a direct quote; I've simply used the Can Can's form and style. It's not necessary for the performer to know this in order to perform the work. If played properly, the rhythms and dynamics will convey it. What's really important, however, is that the performer develops a sense of excitement and energy while playing.

Musical form creates a sense of organization for the listener. Themes return as old friends—they are welcome, recognizable, and comfortable to be with. Variation increases interest and anticipation. Themes may return with a slightly different or drastic change, but should always have a sense of being familiar.

OBSERVATIONS:

1. Begin the opening *fp* roll as a small explosion (as opposed to the lightness and crispness of the following eighth notes). As a performer, imagine the "Can Can" music; try to recreate this same boisterous character.
2. Notice the *staccato* marks on the eighth notes which indicate a short, dry stroke. Use a slight accent here.
3. The last three measures of line 3 begin with a series of loud and soft dynamics. These measures should be played closer to the center of the drum, moving only slightly off-center for softer passages (this will keep the sound consistent).
4. The *fp* in line 4 is a deceptive marking since both sixteenth notes are actually played at the *forte* level. As in the beginning, the *piano* begins on the *staccato* notes.
5. The pick-up notes, into line 6, begin a theme starting on the up-beat. This theme conforms to the opening phrase (also an up-beat). Since the notes are tied over the barline, the notation may seem a bit unusual. I usually don't recommend this notation, but I have included it here as a challenge. Be sure to phrase according to the notation. The natural accent comes on the up-beat and not the down-beat. A simpler way of notating these measures is as follows:

INTERPRETATIONS:

1. Play the entire opening section near the center of the head, moving slightly off-center for the *staccato* notes. I suggest the opening roll be played as a closed 5-stroke roll. To avoid unnecessary doubling into the rolls, try the following sticking pattern:

2. Observe the notation of measure four of line 6, and notice the eighth-note roll tied to an eighth note—and then tied to another eighth note. This may appear to be an error, but it is not. Play it as a 5-stroke roll tied to the last eighth note of the measure. This eighth note is then tied to the first note of the fifth measure; in other words, it is not articulated. Think of the first note of measure five as an eighth-note rest.
3. Separate the series of rolls beginning at the end of line 8, allowing each one to start as written, with a fresh accent. The danger here is to <u>end</u> each roll with an accent. If this is done, additional notes, not written, are added. For best results, think of ending each roll with a slight rest before beginning a new one.

18

Scherzo ♩ = 160

ETUDE #19

A study of musical form is presented in Etude #19, providing us with a sampling of the book's second section. An Introduction begins with the opening Largo, leading to the first theme (A) the Vivace. An introduction should do exactly what it suggests—introduce the main body of the work. In this case, it is done in dramatic fashion by using wedge accents. A smooth transition into the vivace is also created with a simple rhythm modulation. In line 3, the sixteenth and thirty-second-note rhythms of the Introduction become the eighth and sixteenth notes of the new tempo.

The body of the work contains an A theme (Vivace) and a B theme—the B theme begins after the repeat in line 5. There is a similar rhythm modulation in the last two lines as the transition is made from the B section to a restatement of the Introduction. Analyzing musical form, an important element of every composition, helps to understand the composer's intentions, and also aids in memorization.

OBSERVATIONS:

1. Wedge accents (in the opening) help emphasize and exaggerate the Introduction's character. Notice the normal accents in line 2; less energy is needed here. Be sure to focus on the transition being made into the Vivace.

2. In lines 6, 7, and 8, accents are placed on the ends of the short rolls—with one exception, line 7, measure two. This is not a mistake; the final accent in the series of eighth-note rolls is reversed and placed on the roll.

3. "Augmentation", a compositional device repeating a theme or phrase twice as slow, is used in line 7, measure four, and line 8, measure two.

INTERPRETATIONS:

1. Important notes within the Introduction are clearly indicated by the opening accents. To effectively execute these accents, be sure the note following the roll (the release of the roll) is not articulated with an accent.

2. The transition from the opening Largo into the Vivace is written as a simple double-time process; that is, the speed of the sixteenth and thirty-second notes in the Largo is exactly the same as the eighth and sixteenth notes in the Vivace. Given a performer's creative liberties, however, I perform this transition using a slight increase at the Vivace. The new section (A theme) is thus set apart from the transition and the beginning of the theme is more readily heard. Performer's should be sensitive to what listeners are hearing and adjust the music accordingly. Performances vary because of the performer's interpretations.

3. Exaggerate the end of the *crescendo* in line 5, immediately before the repeat. This way, as the first theme is repeated, the *subito p* dynamic will be emphasized.

4. Notice the dotted quarter-note roll in line 5, measure 3; it is followed by a drag. Release this roll early in order to prepare for the drag.

5. Observe the G.P. in line 8. This is an abbreviation for Grand Pause (or General Pause)—actually, it is a measure of silence. It is incorrect to treat it as a *fermata* or a hold. This indication is very helpful, especially in orchestral music, because each player knows no one else will play here. Simply count the correct number of beats in the rest. Beethoven cleverly used this as a device at the end of movements so players would not move until the piece was over!

19

ETUDE #20

Etude #20 provides an opportunity to discuss the subject of METRIC MODULATION. Melodic modulations are used when making a transition from one key (or mode) to another. Metric modulations are used to describe passages from one tempo to another.

In the example below, the composer allows the previous eighth-note value to equal the following quarter-note value:

Instead of changing tempo by increasing or decreasing the speed of the notes, the tempo is adjusted by allowing one note value to become the value of another. In the example above, the value of the eighth note in 4/4 time becomes the value of the quarter note in 3/4 time—causing the tempo to become twice as fast. The cue notes between the measures indicate this change.

Another, more involved example below, shows the value of the triplet eighth note in 2/4 time becoming the value of the eighth note in 4/4 time. This also causes an increase in tempo.

The use of superimposed rhythms (those rhythms that do not divide equally over a beat) may provide an even more complicated example. The value of the quintuplet eighth note in 4/4 time becomes the value of the triplet eighth note in 2/4 time. The tempo is slightly increased.

A method of changing the tempo (pulse) by adjusting the speed (or time value) of a given note has just been discussed. The speed of the notes can also be adjusted without changing the tempo (or pulse) by allowing the tempo of one time signature to become the tempo of another time signature. The following example is taken from line 3 of Etude #20:

The cue notes tell us that the value (or tempo) of the quarter note becomes the value of the dotted quarter note. This places six, sixteenth notes within the space of four, sixteenth notes. The speed of the sixteenth notes is, therefore, increased. The tempo (or pulse) remains the same. The foot tap remains constant during this metric change.

Instead of a metric change, triplets can be used to increase note speed. Both methods accomplish the same goal—they increase the number of notes per beat.

Although the speed of the notes is increased by the same ratio, a change in phrasing occurs when using triplets. Play the first example of line 3 as originally written; then, play the above example. Can you feel the different phrasing? It is important for composers to take this into consideration when using these techniques.

OBSERVATIONS:

1. The tempo marking is listed as 72 to the dotted quarter note. Although metronome markings do not always coincide with phrase groups, in this case, the dotted quarter-note pulse should also become the phrase emphasis. In order to properly phrase the music, place a slight accent on the beginning of each group of notes.

2. Remember, in line 2 the tempo stays the same—only the note values change.

3. A series of grace notes (flams, drags, 4-stroke ruffs, 5- and 7-stroke rolls) begin at the end of line 3. I suggest ending all figures with the strong hand—keeping the sound consistent.

4. Be careful of the sixteenth-note value at the end of lines 9 and 10. There is a metric modulation between these lines and the sixteenth values are different.

INTERPRETATIONS:

1. Treat both *crescendo* markings in line 3 the same. Start line 3 at a *piano* marking to coincide with the second measure.

2. I encourage creative liberties when performing solo literature. Place a short comma or *pausa* after the 7-stroke roll at the end of line 4. This momentarily holds the tension from the *fortissimo* ruffs and sets apart the following *piano* section.

3. Phrase each group of three beats with a slight, natural accent throughout lines 5, 6, and 7. This will change the emphasis; especially, in lines 6 and 7. In line 6, the emphasis will shift from the beginning of a group of notes to the middle, and end as follows:

Line 7 also has changing emphasis as the rhythms shift around the beats.

4. Right-handed players should use the following sticking for the last line so the final note of all the patterns ends with the strong hand (reverse for left-handed players).

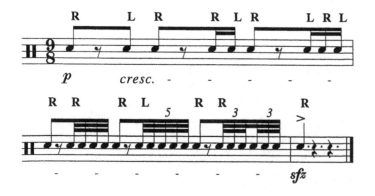

20

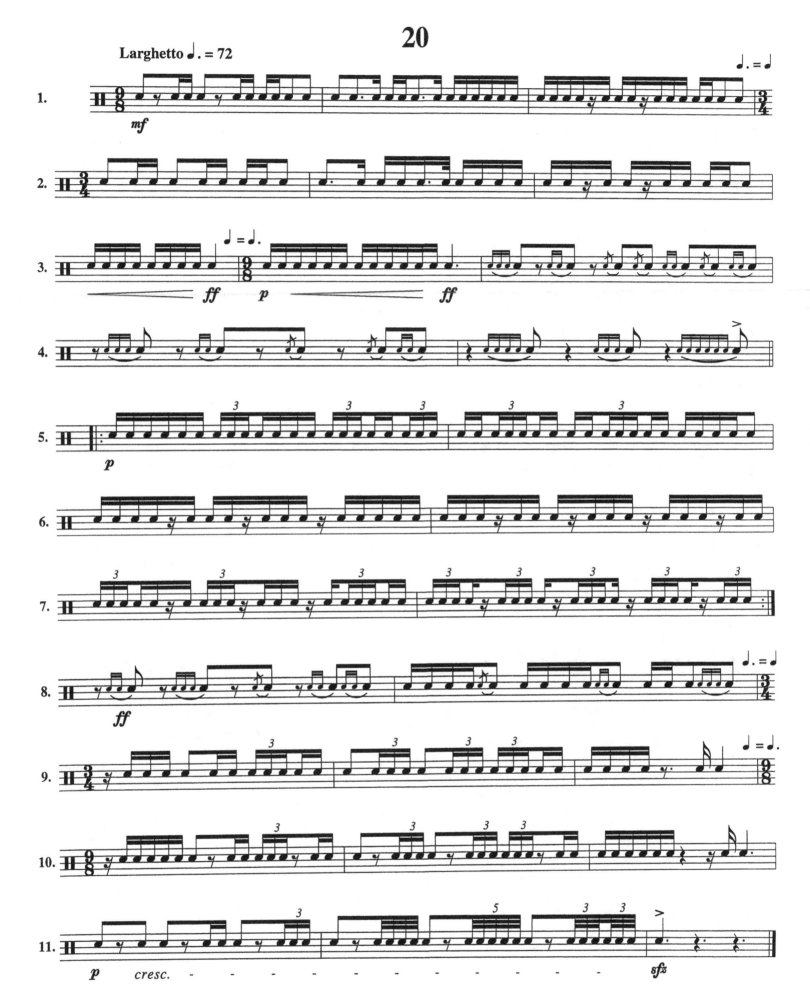

ETUDE #21

Etude #21 addresses the subject of mixed meter. I suggest reviewing Etude #17 if there are any remaining questions regarding the counting from one meter to another. A few basic rules for counting mixed-meter time signatures are as follows:

1. The bottom number of the time signature determines which note receives the main beat. In Etude #21, it is the eighth note.

2. Always count the proper number of beats (determined by the top number of the time signature).

3. Maintain the proper counting relationship between quarter-note, eighth-note, and sixteenth-note rhythms. In this piece, for example, since the eighth note receives the main count (as the quarter note would in 4/4 time), the sixteenth notes are counted as eighth notes.

Now that we have discussed the proper way of counting these rhythms, let's concern ourselves with the main reason a composer writes in mixed meters—that is, phrasing. The following is a simple example of straight eighth notes in 5/8 time:

When a composer arranges the order of notes, as above, s/he expects a slight accent on each group of notes. This shifts the pattern from 3 and 2 in the first measure, to 2 and 3 in the second measure, etc. When these natural accents are not added to the 5/8 pattern, the rhythms may sound as though they were written in an "even" time signature such as 4/4 time.

If this principle is applied to Etude #21, we see the phrasing in measure one is different from measure three since the order of notes has been reversed from 4 and 3 to 3 and 4. This concept can be applied to almost all examples where shifting patterns of rhythm occur throughout the measures. An exception may occasionally be found in orchestral parts where steady articulation is desired even though patterns are changing; this would occur because of other considerations in the music. Percussion notation is not always clear, therefore, orchestral players must constantly listen to the orchestra to determine correct phrasing. In solo music, such as Etude #21, a performer may take creative liberties with phrasing.

OBSERVATIONS:

1. Remember, the symbol written between measures one and two (eighth note = eighth note), tells us that the eighth note is constant throughout the metric changes.

2. Look at line 2 and notice that the notation in the first two measures does not give us a clear indication of phrasing. Some possibilities for the first measure are: 3-2-2, 2-3-2, or 3-4. The second measure may be phrased as follows: 3-2-2, 3-4, or 4-3. When I play this Etude, I phrase these two measures as 2-3-2 and 3-2-2. I find it a good discipline to tap my foot on all phrasing points. Tapping the foot also helps to emphasize phrasing.

3. Play the short *crescendos* at the end of line 6 in the center of the head. Quick changes between dynamics do not sound as effective when moving from the edge to the center.

INTERPRETATIONS:

1. In keeping with the opening discussion, add a slight natural accent to the beginning of all groups of notes.

2. The accent at the end of line 1 creates a dramatic dynamic change into the following *piano*. I suggest exaggerating this accent and then suddenly moving to the edge of the head for the next two measures.

3. The series of rolls in line 3 are not tied together and each roll should have a separate attack. Be careful not to end the rolls with an articulated sound or accent.

4. I suggest playing the series of flams in line 4 with the same hand. An exception may be applied to this rule when it is not necessary for the flams to sound the same; for example, when they are separated by a barline. The reason for this is because the downbeat of the measure has a natural accent and the need to have both flams sound the same is not necessary. In this case, there are two instances when the flam on the downbeat is preceded by another flam (measures two and four); either sticking will work in these measures.

5. In line 8, the *decrescendo* sometimes acts as a phrase marking and is an indication to play the entire measure as one phrase—that is, without adding a natural accent on the last group of four notes. In order to be consistent with the rest of the piece, however, I suggest adding the natural accent at this point.

6. The last measure of line 8 has two sets of thirty-second notes. It seems that students who have a strong rudimental background want to play thirty-second notes as double strokes. I do not advise this because it is difficult to play double strokes as evenly as single strokes. The thirty-second-note rhythms, as with other rhythms, should be alternated.

21

Presto ma non troppo ♪ = 184

ETUDE #22

Etude #22 provides us with an opportunity to discuss superimposed rhythms. These rhythms have more (or less) than the normal configuration of notes within a beat. Any amount of notes can be superimposed over a given beat or beats by placing a number over the grouped notes.

This technique is commonly found in contemporary music because it allows the composer to create unusual rhythmical patterns. Rhythms of this type characterize some of the strongest differences between Classical and Contemporary music. The composer is also able to create a feeling of non-meter by connecting different superimposed rhythms.

The following is a very simple example of a superimposed rhythm:

Triplets are rarely thought of as superimposed rhythms because they are so common; however, by using them, the composer is able to place three notes in the space of two. In the above example, there are two eighth notes to the beat. When using a triplet, three eighth notes are now placed within the space of two, causing the speed of the triplet eighth note to be faster than the normal eighth note.

Some additional examples of superimposing three notes over the space of two are as follows:

The reverse is also possible by placing two notes over the space of three—this is what happens in Etude #22. In the fourth beat of measure one, line 2, there are two eighth notes with a number 2 over them; these notes are played over the fourth beat, which normally has three eighth notes.

Another example used in Etude #22 is found in the second measure of line 3. In this case, a group of five notes are placed over the space of three notes.

This same group of five notes can be played in 4/4 time over 4 notes.

Observe how complicated this can become when rests and ties are placed within the five-note groups.

A typical example of superimposed rhythms is taken from *"Déjà Vu"* For Percussion Quartet and Orchestra by Michael Colgrass.

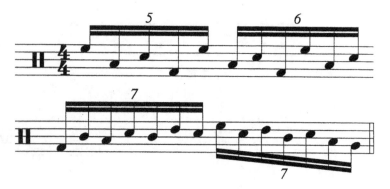

The following measure is written for four drums and should present a challenge. The key (below) may be of some help.

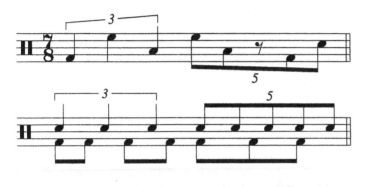

OBSERVATIONS:

1. Measure two begins with three dotted eighth notes and a dotted eighth rest. Count this measure as follows:

This notation accomplishes exactly what the superimposed rhythms do in line 2; two notes are placed over the space of three notes. It is simply another way to notate the same effect. The last measure of line 2 places these rhythms together. The first half of this measure creates a syncopated effect; the superimposed notation does not. Count this measure in the following manner to feel the difference:

2. Line 4 has a simple metric modulation from 12/8 to 2/4. The indication above the measures denotes the fact that the eighth notes remain constant. I suggest counting these measures in the following manner:

3. The final observation of this Etude has to do with the *accelerando* at the end of the piece. The *accelerando* takes place over four measures. A common mistake students make is to change the tempo suddenly at each measure—this is not the proper effect. The pulse should gradually change over the entire four measures, reaching a rapid pace two measures before the end.

INTERPRETATIONS:

1. In Observation #1, I mentioned the syncopated effect that takes place when writing dotted eighth notes. When performing this Etude, I suggest avoiding that feeling—play both the dotted notes and the superimposed notes as a duple.

2. The flams, in the last measure of line 1, create a phrase beginning on the second eighth note. This is the proper way to phrase this measure.

3. The *pianissimo* section, beginning at line 5, is very difficult. First of all, it's not easy to see these rhythms because of note and rest placement. For ease in reading this passage, mark the main beats in the 6/8 and 12/8 measures. Use a very slow, soft roll to avoid unwanted accents. Also, use one hand in the 6/8 and 12/8 measures to keep the notes as even as possible.

4. In the final five measures, the tempo gets faster and the notes get slower. This is the proper effect for the ending. The final five dotted quarter notes should be slower than the sixteenth notes in line 8; however, the actual tempo will be faster.

5. The *fermata* over the rest in the last measure is very important. It creates a moment of silence between the tremendous *accelerando* and the final soft *piano* roll that ends the piece. If this moment is **too long**, the tension of the *accelerando* will be lost. In the same respect, it cannot be **too short** or the effect of the roll (the release of built-up tension) will not be accomplished.

22

This page has been left blank to facilitate page turns.

ETUDE #23

Etude #23 begins the second section of Portraits in Rhythm. The first section contained twenty two solos for snare drum with an emphasis on PHRASING, DYNAMICS, INTERPRETATION, and TECHNIQUE. These four areas will continue to be important throughout the book, however, Etudes #23 through #32 will also include Classical musical forms.

Musical form gives a composition cohesiveness. It also contributes character to each work and distinguishes one piece from another. There is also a compositional device called "through composed"; it does not refer to any particular form. It, too, gives a composition a particular shape and character. The Classical forms of music composition that were common during the 18th and 19th centuries have created a wealth of sonatas, symphonies, concertos, and solos that can still be heard in today's concert halls.

The second section of Portraits in Rhythm contains the following musical forms: ABA, Sonatina, Song and Trio, Rondo, Allemande, Courante, Sarabande, Gigue, Theme and Variations, and Sonata Allegro. Each form creates a different character; however, the use of thematic material and variation is common to all the pieces.

The Classical composers used harmonic modulations when moving from one section to another. If a work began in C major, for example, a transition into the second section might be accomplished by modulating from C major to G major. Because these are rhythmic solos and not melodic, I have used rhythmic modulations instead of melodic; that is, instead of modulating from C major to G major, I modulated from 4/4 time to 3/4 time. As I discuss each etude, I will point these out.

OBSERVATIONS:

1. The first theme (A) occurs over measures 1 to 6. Notice the shape of this theme; two measures *forte,* two measures *piano,* then again, two measures *forte.* Be careful of the dotted sixteenth and thirty-second-note rhythms. As I have warned before, whenever dotted rhythms occur with triplets rhythms, the dotted rhythms should be played very short so they do not sound like triplets.

2. The second theme (B) begins at the double bar in measure 7; notice the different time signature (2/4). As I mentioned above, it represents a change in key signature that might have taken place if the Etude was written for a melodic instrument such as the violin or flute. The B theme is very different from the A theme; rhythms are syncopated with heavy accents—this contrasts the flowing triplets in theme A. Notice the wedge accents—they are played with more emphasis than normal accents.

3. In line 6, measure two, the 4/4 measure begins a short transition back to the A theme. The changing time signatures suggest a modulation back to the original time signature of 4/4.

4. Notice the Coda in line 10—it represents closing music and does not add to the form. Usually, a Coda consists of material that has been taken from the body of the work. Also, notice the *più f* marking at this point; the word *più* (Italian) means "more"—therefore, this marking means "louder" and is interpreted as somewhere between *forte* and *fortissimo.*

INTERPRETATIONS:

1. Play the *pianissimo* section in line 5 near the edge of the head to obtain a delicate, as well as, a soft quality to the sound.

2. Once, again, do not alternate flams in line 6. The exception to this may be in measure three of line 6 where a flam-tap sticking can be used.

3. The last line of the piece is written as a traditional classical ending. One hand may be used for the eighth, quarter, and half notes.

4. The final measure is a whole-note roll preceded by a flam. I suggest playing all flams that are attached to rolls on the open side—notice the accent is on the flam.

23

ETUDE #24

This Etude is titled "Sonatina" which is defined as the largest, two-part musical construction. Simply, it means the work is divided into two main sections. The first section begins with an exposition (or primary theme), and moves through a "bridge-like" transition into a secondary theme (in a different key), and concludes with a Coda. The second theme begins in the original key with a recapitulation (or repetition) of the opening theme. A transitory passage leads into the secondary theme, also in the original key. The ending may or may not have a Coda.

Let's now look at Etude #24 to see how this music reflects the Sonatina form. The opening theme consists of the first four measures with measures five, six, and seven functioning as a transition into a secondary theme. Remember from Etude #23, instead of changing the key signature, the time signature was changed. Therefore, the second theme is in a new time signature of 3/8. The second theme begins in line 4 and consists of twelve measures. The last measure of line 5 begins a short transition and the first section ends at the *fermata* in line 6.

The second section begins at the double bar in line 6 and simply restates the opening theme. This time the transition into the second theme consists of seven measures, beginning in line 8, measure two, with a series of sixteenth notes in mixed meters.

The second theme returns in line 9, measure five, but this time it is written in 5/4 instead of 3/8. This is to simulate the original form of the Sonatina where the second theme returns in the original key. In this case, the original key (or time signature) is 5/4. The second theme is extended a bit from the original statement and then leads into the final Coda, which takes on the rhythm of a typical Classical ending.

OBSERVATIONS:

1. Instead of a tempo marking indication such as Allegro or Adagio, this etude has the form name as an indication. This happens at times and, therefore, we are not given any clues to help us in our interpretation. The metronome marking of quarter note = 88 indicates the speed, but nothing helps with the character. Since the Sonatina is a traditional Classical form, I suggest a straightforward, accurate reading of the dynamics with phrasing over each full measure.

2. The proper way to count the mixed-meter measures in line 8, measure two, is as follows:

3. In the section where the second theme comes back in the original time signature (line 9, measure five), the phrasing changes considerably. When this theme was in 3/8, every group of three eighth notes were phrased. Now that it is written in 5/4, every group of two eighth notes is phrased.

INTERPRETATIONS:

1. The first two quarter-note rolls are untied and each one has an accent. Separate the rolls as written and be careful not to articulate the end of each roll with a stroke.

2. The second beat of measure two begins with a short roll—this is not a thirty-second note indication. As I have mentioned, all notes with three slashes are to be executed as rolls unless they have dots to indicate abbreviated notes.

3. The transition in line 3, at the 3/8, presents a problem I have mentioned quite often. That is, when triplets are written along with dotted notes, be sure the dotted notes are played on the short side in order to avoid any feeling of a triplet.

4. The *fermata* on the roll at the double bar in line 6 indicates that the roll should be held. Since there is no rest after this note and there is also no *fermata* on the double barline, there should not be any rest or silence after the roll. At the end of the *fermata,* simply take a breath between the two rolls—then continue.

5. Line 8, measure two, begins a series of sixteenth notes in mixed meters. Phrase both groups of notes in the 2/4 measure, not just the full measure. I treat this measure as though it were two 1/4 measures; in this way, all the groups of sixteenth notes are phrased alike.

24

ETUDE #25

The Song and Trio form is similar to the Sonatina except for the middle (Trio) section. The first section consists of a primary and secondary theme. The Trio follows and separates the return (or recapitulation) of the first two themes. The last two measures form a small Coda or closing music.

The first theme in 6/8 time is from measures one through eight, followed by the second theme, measures nine through fourteen. The Trio begins on line 4 at the 3/4. Take note of the tempo change that helps to set this section apart. The recapitulation begins in line 7 with the indication, Tempo I; this means *tempo primo* (return to the original tempo). The first two themes are repeated without any variation.

OBSERVATIONS:

1. The opening theme begins with the tempo marking indication of Moderato, and the dotted quarter note = 60. The Trio has a marking of Piú allegro (faster)—the Italian word *piú* means "more".

2. Just a reminder, the sixteenth notes with a slash, in lines 2 and 8, refer to rolls and not thirty-second notes.

3. To keep the character of the form, all flams, drags, and 4-stroke ruffs should be on the closed side and very light.

4. There are no dynamic mark changes in the last two measures of the piece. However, because they follow the last statement of the second theme, set them apart by exaggerating the accents—especially the final wedge accent.

INTERPRETATIONS:

1. I add accents to the first two notes of the piece because they provide more energy and excitement to the work. Sometimes the whole character of a performance is set by the opening few bars.

2. Play the *decrescendo* and *crescendo,* in the first line, in the center area of the head. There can be a slight movement towards the edge of the head as the roll gets softer, and then back to the center as it gets louder—but only <u>slightly</u>.

3. There should be a noticeable change of tempo at the Trio. It is preferable that the tempo be faster than indicated, then to be so slight that it goes unnoticed. Also, phrase in one to keep the feeling of a Waltz.

4. Just as the change of tempo at the Trio is important, so is the return in line 7 to the original tempo. Again, add accents to the first two notes and exaggerate the slower tempo change.

Song and Trio

25

ETUDE #26

As the tempo mark indicates, this Etude is in a form called Third Rondo. A Rondo form consists of a principle theme, alternately played with several subordinate themes or episodes. Episodes are always in keys other than the original in Classical music. For our purposes, the key change is represented by a time signature change.

Etude #26, which is technically in a Third Rondo form, has an original theme (which repeats four times) and two episodes. The first episode also returns in the original time signature (line 9, measure two).

OBSERVATIONS:

1. As in previous etudes, the tempo marking describes the form of the work; but, no indication is given as to its character. The metronome marking does show a fast eighth note pulse; so, keep the rhythms light and quick.

2. Line 3 shows an eighth = eighth marking that will alter the pulse from a dotted quarter note to a quarter note. This marking reverses in the fourth measure of line 4.

3. The sixteenth = sixteenth marking at the second measure of line 6 indicates that the speed of the sixteenth notes is equal.

4. The Rondo theme always returns with a *forte* dynamic and dominates the Etude. All the other episodes are marked *mezzo forte* or less. The one exception is the end of the 5/16 episode, which also ends at the *forte* dynamic. Reinforce the *forte* of the theme that follows so it will be heard as a new entrance and not as an extension of the previous music.

INTERPRETATIONS:

1. All the short eighth and sixteenth-note rolls should be measured to insure a solid rhythmical feeling. I suggest a 5-stroke roll for all sixteenth-note rolls, and a 7-stroke roll for all eighth-note rolls.

2. Remember do **not** alternate the multiple drags in lines 3 and 9; but **do** use alternate sticking from a single stroke into all flams and drags. A good way to practice this Etude is to first play the passage hand to hand without the flams or drags—then add the flams and drags as written, using the same sticking.

3. The 5/16 episode is counted in five. Count as indicated below for the thirty-second notes in the final four measures.

26

Third Rondo ♪ = 160

ETUDE #27

The next four etudes are composed in the style of an 18th century dance suite. The first movement, Allemande, is a German dance characterized by a moderate 4/4 tempo. A quick upbeat and frequent use of short, running figures are also prominent in an Allemande.

OBSERVATIONS:

1. The last note of lines 4 and 6 is the pickup note into the theme. The pickup note in line 4 is still in the *forte* dynamic and, in fact, all the pickup notes should have a slight accent to "kick" off the music. This is especially true of the last note on line 6 when played the second time. When this note goes into line 7, the dynamic changes to a *forte* and this note should reflect the dynamic change.

2. The sixteenth-note rolls in line 10 are tied and should be played as closed 5-stroke rolls. This is the shortest tied roll possible. Do not use a one-handed roll because this will sound like a drag.

3. Notice the first roll in measure one of line 7 is not tied into the <u>an</u> of 3, but all the succeeding rolls are tied.

INTERPRETATIONS:

1. Although there are no phrasing marks indicated, the rhythm should flow within the phrases of two and four beats. An example of the first four measures is as follows:

2. Try the following sticking in measures two and three of line 4 to secure accurate off beats.

3. The flam passage starting the second measure of line 8 may be played as a flam and stroke; however, I do recommend using the flam tap sticking on fast passages such as this.

4. The short, untied eighth-note rolls in line 10 are crush rolls and should be played with both sticks pressing into the head simultaneously.

27

Allemande ♩ = 108

ETUDE #27

The Courante is an old French dance usually played in a lively 3/4 or 3/2 tempo. This dance also begins with an upbeat.

OBSERVATIONS:

1. The original Portraits in Rhythm book does not have an accent on the first pickup note or in the first and second measures of line 4. As you can see, this has been corrected and now all the upbeats are played in a similar manner.

2. The normal rule for playing flams or drags in succession is to play them with the same hand for consistency. The exception is when a barline separates the flams as in measure four of line 7, and measure two of line 8. Alternating the flam over the barline is acceptable when the downbeat of a measure needs a slight accent for the start of a phrase.

Line 7, meas. 3 and 4.

Line 8, meas. 1 and 2.

3. The accents on the flams in line 9 are called "wedge" accents and are considerably stronger than a normal accent.

INTERPRETATIONS:

1. Use one hand for all the notes in the first three measures of line 2 for consistency of sound.

2. The roll from the fourth measure of line 2 into the fifth measure is purposely not tied. This allows the following eighth note to sound as the start of a phrase and not the end of the roll.

3. Use alternating sticking in the second and third measures of line 3. Do not play flam-a-diddles.

4. Notice the *diminuendo* to *pppp* in line 7. This indication is asking for as soft a sound as possible.

5. When a phrase is written over the barline, as in measures three and four of line 8, do not accent the downbeat of the measure.

28

ETUDE #29

The Sarabande is a stately, dignified dance in a slow, triple meter. There is usually a prolonged tone or an accent on the second beat.

OBSERVATIONS:

1. The third line begins a series of dotted sixteenth and thirty-second notes. This is a change of character from the opening theme and needs to be played with tight, crisp strokes.

2. Use the edge of the head for the series of drags in lines 6 and 7—this will produce a soft, delicate sound.

3. Do not tie the roll in the final measure. This allows the final two notes to stand alone.

INTERPRETATIONS:

1. The accent on the rolls in the first line should be more of a broad *tenuto* than a sharp attack. This fits better with the stately manner of the Sarabande.

2. The second measure of line 4 has a *crescendo* within a *crescendo*. Drop down on the third beat of the second measure where the hairpin *crescendo* begins to effectively play this second *crescendo*. A more accurate indication of the dynamics is as follows:

3. For right-handed players, the following sticking is suggested for the second and third measures of line 7.

29

ETUDE #30

A lively movement always concluded a dance suite; in this case, a Gigue or Jig is played in triple time.

OBSERVATIONS:

1. Line 7 begins a *pianissimo* section with dotted sixteenth and thirty-second-note rhythms against sixteenth-note triplets. Play the thirty-second notes on the short side to avoid having them sound like triplets.

2. The amount of *decrescendo* in line 11 is left up to the discretion of the performer. Whatever dynamic is chosen, start the *fortissimo* in the center of the head and only move slightly towards the edge for the *decrescendo*.

3. Once again notice the "wedge" accents on the final three notes. These accents should be quite loud in the *fortissimo* dynamic.

INTERPRETATIONS:

1. Although the normal phrasing for 9/8 time would be three groups of 3 beats, the use of the flams cause the phrasing of the opening measures to sound like a 2-2-2-3 grouping. A more accurate way of notating this is as follows:

2. Choose a sensitive spot near the edge of the snare drum head for the *pianissimo* section starting in line 7. Try to play the entire section (including the flam strokes) without accents.

30

Gigue ♩. = 88

ETUDE #31

A Theme and Variation form is exactly what it says: a theme followed by any number of variations. In this case, the Andante theme is followed by: Variation I – Ornamentation, Variation II – Waltz Tempo, Variation III – A fast *Tocatta*, Variation IV – March Tempo, and Variation V – A slow variation called Adagio pesante.

OBSERVATIONS:

1. The opening theme starts simply enough with a six-measure rhythmic melody in 4/4 time.

2. Variation I is identical to the opening theme; except for the ornamentation on the flams, drags, 4 stroke ruffs, and 5-stroke roll.

3. The rhythm pattern changes in Variation II, but the original theme can still be heard in the Waltz.

4. The Allegro Variation is a series of rapid sixteenth notes with accents punctuating the thematic rhythm.

5. Variation IV provides a marching character to the theme.

6. The final Variation is identical in rhythm to the original theme, but the added rolls and slow tempo drastically change its character. The *pesante* indication asks for a "heavy" feeling to the music.

INTERPRETATIONS:

1. The strokes that follow the rolls in the opening theme should be articulated so the note is heard as a strong part of the rhythm.

2. Play all the rudiments in Variation II in a closed "orchestral" manner. These grace notes add a flourish to the Andante character.

3. The Waltz Variation is written in two eight-measure phrases with a three-measure extension at the end. Accent the last measure of line 5 to emphasize the beginning of the second phrase.

4. First practice Variation III without the accents; then, use a slightly larger stroke for all accented notes.

5. The March Variation should have a strong feeling of two pulses to the measure.

6. Separate all the rolls in Variation V. The rolls marked with a *staccato* are played as two-handed crush rolls. The *staccato* on the single strokes requires a slight accent.

Theme and Variations

31

ETUDE #32

The Sonata Allegro form is the largest two-part construction in music. The outline of this form is as follows: Optional Introduction, Exposition, Development, Recapitulation, and an optional Coda. In Etude #32, the Introduction is found in the first two lines. The Exposition begins on line 3 and ends with a transition into the 6/8 in line 7, which begins the secondary theme. The *forte* in line 10 begins the Development section and leads to the Recapitulation in line 15. The return of the secondary theme (in the original meter of the first theme) begins on line 19 with rapid thirty-second notes in line 22, acting as the final Coda.

OBSERVATIONS:

1. The opening tempo marking should more accurately say Moderato misterioso. Try to create this mysterious character by playing the first two measures very slowly (almost out of tempo) and, then, gradually add the *accelerando* and *crescendo*.

2. The speed of the eighth notes remains equal from the 6/8 time into the 4/4 time.

3. The indication of the eighth = eighth in line 7 is a bit deceiving since the *ritard* takes us into a new tempo. A slight pause before the Andante helps to separate the entrance of the secondary theme.

4. Notice the *tenuto* marks on the rolls after the repeat in line 8; they indicate a broad accent on each roll.

5. Even though the dotted eighth = eighth indication at the Presto in line 12 tells us the pulse of the 9/16 is the same as the pulse of the 3/8, the start of the Presto should have the feeling of a brighter tempo.

6. The dotted half note equals the dotted quarter note in line 18, showing the speed of the entire 3/4 measure equals the three eighth notes of the 3/8 measure. This causes the tempo to be twice as slow.

INTERPRETATIONS:

1. The *accelerando* and *crescendo* in line 2 may be interpreted in a number of ways and not necessarily where indicated—be creative!

2. The downbeat of the Presto vivo in line 3 needs an accent to "kick off" this section.

3. The 4/4 phrasing of the Presto vivo should not be played straight; phrase the grouping of notes in a musical manner. An example of this is as follows:

4. The Andante in line 7 also says *grazioso* (gracefully). The *grazioso* can be accomplished by adding a natural phrase of two beats to the measure.

5. All the *staccato* dots in lines 8, 9, and 10 are played by adding a slight accent to the note.

6. Phrase all the note groupings in the mixed-meter section in line 12—not just the downbeats.

7. The Presto vivo returns in line 15 and should be in the same tempo as line 3. To accomplish this, the previous Presto in line 12 must be played slower than the Presto vivo tempo in line 15.

8. When the Andante grazioso returns in line 19, the time signature changes to 4/4, causing the phrasing to be quite different (as indicated below):

This page has been left blank to facilitate page turns.

32

ETUDE #33

Etude #33 begins the last section of the book. These exercises are similar to the first section with a greater degree of difficulty. Syncopation is stressed in many of the etudes, as in this piece, so pay much attention to the accents.

OBSERVATIONS:

1. It is important not to begin this Etude too fast since there are difficult passages later on.

2. Most of the untied rolls in Etude #33 are to be played as crush rolls. An exception is the last measure of line 4, which is a normal roll, but must be separated from the flam.

3. All crush rolls should be played with both sticks simultaneously striking the head.

4. Sixteenth notes with one slash indicate a crush roll.

5. A dot over a single stroke indicates a slight accent.

INTERPRETATIONS:

1. As a general rule, use alternating sticking when the flams are preceded or followed by a single stroke. Two or more flams played in succession should be played with the same hand (all right- or all left-handed flams).

2. The exceptions are those measures listed below which are more easily played as flam taps:

a. The second measure of line 4.

b. The fourth measure of line 6.

c. Line 10.

33

ETUDE #34

In passages where time signatures interchange regularly, composers often indicate the meters at the beginning of the work and do not bother with a time signature in each measure. This has been done in the following piece where the metric pattern continually alternates between 3/8 and 2/8.

OBSERVATIONS:

1. Place a natural accent on the beginning of each measure to bring out the 3 and 2 patterns. This music will sound very similar to 5/8 with the possible exception that with each measure having its own time signature, the downbeat phrasing will sound equal. In 5/8, the second phrase may not always sound as strong as the downbeat phrase.

2. Notice in line 5 that the pattern reverses after the double bar to a 2 and 3. In the first seven measures after the double bar however, the accents will force the phrases into all groups of 2. If the player continues to tap on the downbeat of each measure, these accents will feel syncopated. The third measure of line 9 reverses once again to the original 3 and 2 phrasing.

3. The last two measures of lines 10 and 11 are beamed over the bar line. Do not accent the downbeat of the second measure in these cases—play both of these measures as one phrase.

INTERPRETATIONS:

1. Do not alternate the flams starting in the last two measures of line 2; however, do place a slight accent on each flam that occurs on the downbeat. This is an interpretive decision that, I believe, works well for solo music. If this passage was written in an orchestral situation, the music may demand that each flam be played equal without the sense of phrasing.

2. The *pianissimo* in line 6 begins a series of steady sixteenth notes, which also need a slight accent on each downbeat of the measures. Retain the *pianissimo* dynamic throughout the accented section and then *crescendo* as indicated.

3. Use alternating sticking with the single strokes and drags starting in measure three of line 9 as follows:

34

Presto ♩. = 88

ETUDE #35

Etude #35 is an excellent study for sub-dividing the eighth note throughout the piece. The extreme slow quarter-note pulse (mm = 48) must be sub-divided to insure rhythmic precision without any feeling of rushing. The opening figure is a good example, because to place the sixteenth note of beat one, the player must feel the <u>an</u> of one. It might even be more accurate to count all the sixteenth sub-divisions of the beat—1,e,an,a.

OBSERVATIONS:

1. The opening 7-stroke roll should be played closed and must land directly on beat one. Therefore, the grace-notes are played as an upbeat. In the second measure, this same figure lands on the second sixteenth of beat one. This 7-stroke roll must actually begin on the downbeat of one to allow enough time to end on the second sixteenth value.

2. Be sure to distinguish between the normal accent and the "wedge" accent (which is played louder).

3. Most of the rolls are tied into the following notes—be sure to articulate all of these strokes. An exception is in the first measure of lines 7 and 10. Both of these measures have a roll that is separated from the succeeding note. This is purposely done to allow the following note a greater degree of importance.

INTERPRETATIONS:

1. Etude #35 contrasts very loud and very soft sections. Use the center of the head for all loud passages and a sensitive area near the edge of the head for all soft passages.

2. In many of the previous Etudes, much has been mentioned about adding phrasing to the music. In this particular Etude, I suggest playing all the soft passages as even and consistent as possible with no accents.

3. Stick the 5/4 measure in line 9 as indicated below to play the offbeats evenly and precise.

4. The roll in the second measure of line 3 is also not tied to the following drag. Rolls that are followed by flams, drags and 4-stroke ruffs are always difficult to play since the roll must not end with an articulated note. Leave a slight space to set up for the grace notes.

35

ETUDE #36

This 6/8 Etude shows how by the use of flams, accents, and the placement of beams, a composer can create unusual patterns within the normal structure of a time signature. The additions of these elements can create shifting phrases and a syncopated feeling throughout the music.

OBSERVATIONS:

1. The flam placement in the opening eight measures shifts the natural pulse of 1 and 4 to an upbeat feeling on 3 and 6. When the flam is used on the second and fourth beats of the measure, a syncopated feeling prevails. A flam forces the phrasing by the weight it adds to the note.

2. Again, in line 4, the addition of the flam and accent forces the phrase from the normal downbeat pulse to the last sixteenth note of each group.

3. Line 6 uses phrase groups of 2, 3, and 4 to replace the normal 6/8 groupings of 3. A slight accent on the beginning of each group is necessary to bring out this phrasing.

INTERPRETATIONS:

1. The last two measures of line 3 consist of a series of sixteenth notes with pairs of accents. Be sure to play these accents hand to hand—do not double these strokes.

2. Try the following stickings starting on the third measure of line 4:

3. When playing lines 6 and 7 as described in Observation #3, tap your foot on the first and third beats of each measures and not on the downbeats of each phrase. This will take some practice, but it is an excellent coordination exercise.

4. I suggest the following sticking patterns beginning in line 9:

36

ETUDE #37

Etude #37 is based on the rhythms of the famous snare drum part in Rimsky-Korsakov's Capriccio Espagnol. This excerpt is from the Alborada III movement and is used quite often in percussion auditions. The actual excerpt is present in the Etude; however, additional material and phrasing is also added.

OBSERVATIONS:

1. The character of the music is march-like and the use of an open-sounding roll is appropriate to create this character and maintain the consistency of the rolls.

2. The second part of this excerpt begins after the double bar in line 4. In the actual part, this music is played directly after the opening nine bars and continues the same character; therefore, all the rolls should have a similar sound.

3. The use of the *staccato* markings is not original to the actual music and is added to help the student with phrasing.

INTERPRETATIONS:

1. Do not play the rolls as actual double-stroke rolls. Just use less multiple bounces to get the march-like character. Below is an example of the passage written out as measured rolls—this indicates the pulse of the rolls, but be sure to use a multiple bounce for each stroke.

*Each sixteenth note receives a multiple-bounce stroke.

2. All the *staccato* dots should be played with a slight accent. This adds an emphasis on the up-beat in the first four lines and gives some life to the music. This would be considered an interpretation of the composer's wishes based on the orchestral music and should not be overdone when playing auditions.

3. Play the middle section, starting after the double bar in line 4, with a *marcato* (with a marked emphasis) feeling by giving equal weight to each note of the triplets.

37

90

ETUDE #38

Probably the most famous snare drum excerpt is from Rimsky Korsakov's Scheherazade. Below are three selected rhythms from the third movement of this work.

OBSERVATIONS:

1. The opening measures are actually the rhythms played by the violins immediately preceding the snare drum entrance. This cue is very important when playing the actual snare drum part with the orchestra in order to come in properly.

2. The notation of the thirty-second notes in the first of the three rhythms beginning in the last measure of line 2, is technically incorrect. The grouping of these 6 notes actually occurs over the second eighth note of the measure and should have a 6 over the beam as written below.

3. The first four measures after the double bar in line 2 are quoted directly from the actual snare drum part. The remaining rhythms until line 6 are a variation. The four measures beginning on line 6 and the seven measures beginning on measure three of line 8 are also actual quotations from the snare drum part.

INTERPRETATIONS:

1. The untied rolls in the second measure are correct—so separate the roll from the following sixteenth note.

2. The sticking indicated after the double bar in line 2 is one of the more common ways to play this part. They are not played using alternating strokes because of the speed of the sextuplets. Using double strokes actually makes this a 7-stroke roll figure; however, the notes must be played absolutely in rhythm and should not sound like a roll. Below is another way of sticking this passage using the same hand on all the eighth notes.

3. The most popular method of playing the second excerpt beginning in line 6 is with a double paradiddle sticking as indicated below.

4. The third excerpt starting in the third measure of line 8 is played by using an open 9-stroke roll. The open character of this roll is consistent with the music written for the other orchestral instruments.

38

ETUDE #39

While mixed-meters are used throughout Portraits in Rhythm, Etude #39 is one of the few that combines quarter, eighth, and sixteenth-note based time signatures. The method of counting these mixed-meter patterns is outlined in Etude #47. Please refer to that Etude for instructions on counting.

OBSERVATIONS:

1. The tempo marking of Andante con vigoroso may seem contradictory; however, the Andante refers more to the actual tempo while the con vigoroso refers to the character of the music (which in this case is quite vigorous).

2. The use of the 3/16 measure reverses the accents in line 3, while in line 11, it reverses the rhythm.

3. The opening theme returns only one time at the *ff* in line 7. This *ff* marking is the loudest in the piece; so, keep the opening *f* level down in anticipation of this measure.

4. Be prepared for the *subito f* on the second measure of line 10. Do not make any *crescendo* on the roll preceding this downbeat.

INTERPRETATIONS:

1. The *crescendo* in the last measure of line 1 only goes to a *forte*. It is necessary, therefore, to drop the dynamic marking down to a *mp* or *mf* at the beginning of the last measure in line 1 to make this effective. Play in a similar manner at the end of line 2. The *crescendo* at the end of line 2 should also go to a *forte*.

2. The speed of the sixteenth notes is equal and the counting for the 3/16 measure in line 3 is as follows:

3. All sixteenth-note rolls that are tied over should be played as closed 5-stroke rolls.

4. Separate the rolls that are not tied in line 6.

5. The eighth and sixteenth-note rolls with dots in line 7 are crush rolls—and, for all practical purposes, are of the same length.

39

Andante con vigoroso ♩ = 84

ETUDE #40

As with all of the mixed-meter solos, phrasing is determined by the grouping of notes. It is also advisable to tap your foot on each group to assist in the phrasing and to develop good hand/foot coordination.

OBSERVATIONS:

1. The use of the flam and drag rudiments alters the phrasing simply by the weight they add to a note. When these rudiments are added, as in the last two measures of line 1, they will receive more weight than the downbeat of each group and provide a syncopated feeling to the measure.

2. The proper counting for line 4 is as follows:

3. The accents and grouping of the last two measures force a duple feel over the barline. If you tap your foot on each group, these two measures will sound as though they are in 2/8 time. However, if you tap your foot as indicated below, the measures will sound syncopated.

INTERPRETATIONS:

1. Try the following sticking for measures five through eight. The alternating sticking provides a consistent sound and utilizes both right and left-handed flams.

2. Similarly, plan ahead in measure three of line five to determine whether the flams and drags that follow will be played on the right or left hand.

3. One of the most difficult passages in Portraits in Rhythm occurs in line 8. I suggest the following sticking and lots of practice.

40

Allegro ma non troppo ♩. = 76

ETUDE #41

Etude #41 is a study in the dotted eighth/sixteenth and triplet relationship. There is a danger when playing a dotted eighth note against a triplet rhythm; that is to not make the sixteenth note sound like a triplet. The sixteenth note should actually be played a bit shorter than normal (closer to a thirty-second note) when preceded or followed by a triplet rhythm.

OBSERVATIONS:

1. The fast tempo contributes to the difficulty of this piece; however, the sixteenth and triplet relationship can be just as much a problem in a slow tempo. With each note lasting for a longer duration, there is more room for error.

2. Since the entire Etude is *pianissimo,* select a spot near the edge of the head that is sensitive, but still has a good of snare sound.

INTERPRETATIONS:

1. Use alternating sticking for all the connecting rhythms. For single notes in sequence, use one hand. Two examples of this sticking can be found in measures three, four, six, and seven.

2. Be sure both sticks strike the snare drum head at the same distance from the rim. If one stick strikes the head closer to the rim than the other, the two strokes will not sound similar.

3. Practice using a slight movement of the wrist when playing *pianissimo.* The idea is to produce repeated identical strokes with no unwanted accents or phrasing.

41

ETUDE #42

Etude #42 is one of the solos I feel is well-suited for competitions and recitals. There are many elements in this work that require a strong technique and musical awareness to be successful.

OBSERVATIONS:

1. The opening tempo mark of Largo tells us this music has the character of a very slow pulse. The con moto reflects the many rapid thirty-second-note rhythms. However, be sure the main pulse is on the quarter note. What is not reflected by the tempo mark is the *maestoso* character that is needed in the opening measures.

2. Etude #42 also contains one of the long *pianissimo* sections, starting in line 3. Try to play all the notes evenly without any feeling of accents or phrasing.

3. Notice, at the end of line 7, where each of the two tied rolls has an accent marking. Do not separate the roll from this accent; simply attack the third beat without breaking the roll.

4. The dotted thirty-second and sixty-fourth-note rhythms, beginning at the end of line 9, must be played quite short and crisp.

INTERPRETATIONS:

1. The accented roll on measure 2 should remain *forte* for a moment before making the *diminuendo*. The danger here is in making this sound like a *fp*. It is also important to articulate the note following the roll to begin this thirty-second-note triplet passage.

2. All **tied** sixteenth-note rolls should be played as closed 5-stroke rolls.

3. The dots on the **untied** eighth and sixteenth-note rolls are to be played as two-handed crush rolls. The dots on the single strokes indicate a *staccato* stroke and should be played with a slight accent.

4. The final measure contains two rolls. One roll on a sixteenth note and the other on a thirty-second note. For all practical purposes, both rolls must be played as closed 5-stroke rolls. The thirty-second-note roll, therefore, will be twice as fast as the sixteenth-note roll. The 5-stroke roll is the shortest roll possible—anything less would sound like a drag.

42

Largo con moto ♩ = 48

This page has been left blank to facilitate page turns.

ETUDE #43

Etude #43 is a typical 9/8 solo with most of the measures divided into three groups of three beats each. This Etude is not as thematic as many others in the book, however the opening measures return, in part, in line 10. The music is more "through-composed," exploring the many variations of 9/8 phrasing.

OBSERVATIONS:

1. Because of the many subdivisions of the nine basic beats, I suggest learning this piece, at first, with nine beats to the measure and, eventually, phrasing the three groups of three beats per measure.

2. The second measure of line 3 is the only measure not phrased in three beats. This measure is actually a 1-2-2-2-2 grouping.

3. Line 7 begins a series of dotted thirty-second and sixty-fourth notes similar to Etude #42. Remember the sixty-fourth note must be quite short and crisp to avoid it sounding like a triplet.

INTERPRETATIONS:

1. Line 3 begins at a *forte* level with a *crescendo* in measure two, building up to a *fortissimo* in measure three. I suggest starting the eighth-note rolls at a *mezzo piano* dynamic to increase the amount of *crescendo* to the *fortissimo* level. This is simply an interpretation of the actual notation and it is up to the creative desire of the performer as to how he or she will play it.

2. The character changes quite a bit in line 7 with the dotted thirty-second and sixty-fourth-note rhythms. It is the softest dynamic of the Etude, yet it has the most driving rhythm of the piece. As mentioned in the Observations, the solution is to keep the rhythms as short and crisp as possible.

3. Starting at line 13, there are three types of rolls in the following three lines: (1). Untied rolls, (2). Tied rolls, (3). Crush rolls. Only rolls with dots should be considered crush rolls. Eighth-note rolls without dots should be played as untied, long rolls.

43

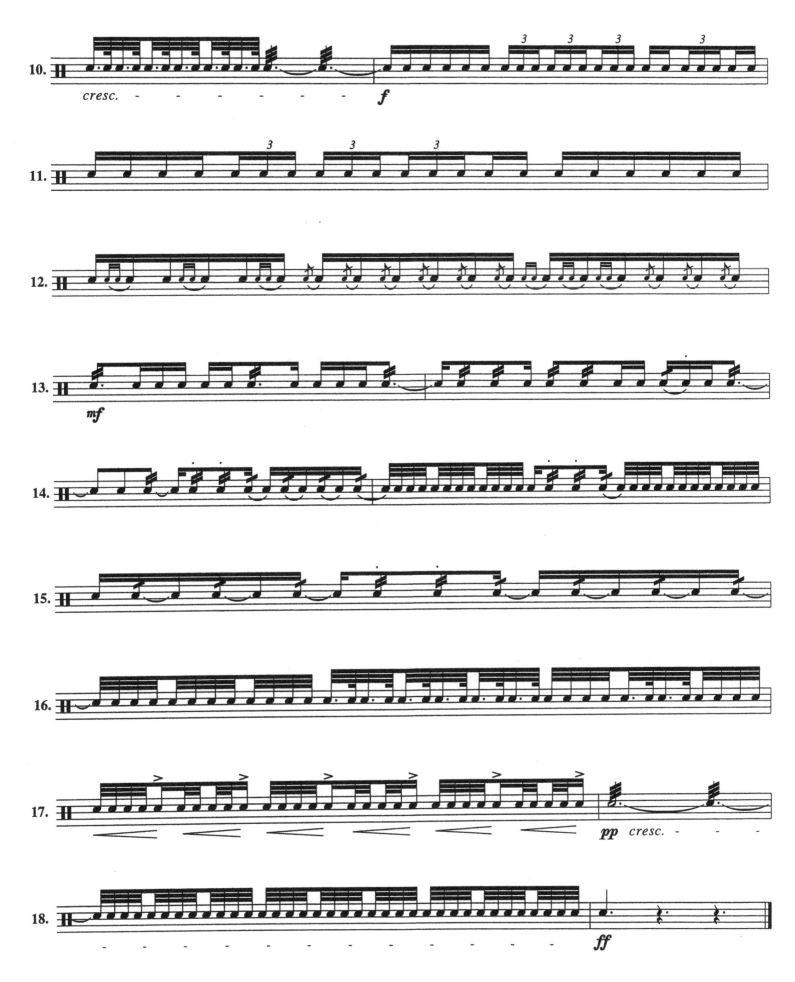

ETUDE #44

Etude #44 uses a combination of many of the elements found in previous etudes. Musically, there is an emphasis on syncopation.

OBSERVATIONS:

1. The Andante refers to the dotted quarter-note pulse. The eighth-note pulse is quite fast and does add a driving force to the music. Maintain the dotted-quarter note feel as the primary phrase while allowing the accents to predominate as written.

2. The end of line 3 begins a series of tiered dynamics. Immediately drop to the next level without any feeling of *decrescendo*.

3. Be particularly careful to play both sixteenth notes and rolls at the *pianissimo* level in line 7. Try to avoid any feeling of accents on the rolls.

INTERPRETATIONS:

1. There are a few places where flams or drags occur at the beginning and end of a 4-note pattern—such as the first measure of line 3. Alternate the strokes into the second flam as indicated below.

2. The rolls in line 7 are **not** tied over to the following note; so, be sure to leave a bit of space between the rolls and the next measure. In line 8, the rolls **are** tied and no separation should be heard. The notes following the rolls, however, **are** meant to be articulated.

3. All of the many series of flams, such as in lines 3, 4, and 10 should be played on the same hand. This is the most secure method of assuring a consistent sound.

44

ETUDE #45

All the time signatures in Etude #45 are sixteenth-note based. When mixed meters have the same denominator, whether a quarter, eighth, or sixteenth note, the counting is relatively simple since the pulse does not change. In this case, every measure is divided into 1,2,3, or 4 sixteenth-note groups.

OBSERVATIONS:

1. The first and last measures combine to make a complete measure. Composers may write "pick-up" notes in this manner or simply write out the rests in both measures. In any case, the music is played the same.

2. The two "pick-up" notes determine the phrasing for the opening measures. The following is a more exact notation for phrasing the first four measures:

3. The remaining measures of the first two lines should be phrased as determined by the beaming.

INTERPRETATIONS:

1. The use of slurs helps clarify how music should be phrased. This is how line 2 would look with slurs:

2. When a phrase extends over the barline, as in measure two, the last note of the phrase should not be accented. Normally, the first note of a measure might receive a slight accent; however, when it is the last note of a phrase, it simply ends with a gentle stroke. The beginning of each phrase, wherever it comes within the measure, needs a slight accent.

3. Since the entire Etude is in some form of a sixteen time, all the counting remains consistent. The sixteenth note receives the main count. The opening measures should be counted as follows:

45

ETUDE #46

Abbreviated rhythmic spelling can be found in the literature for all instruments; however, because of the repetitive nature of percussion music, it is frequently used in percussion notation. Since none of the other Etudes have used this shorthand method, I have written Etude #46 to cover this subject thoroughly.

OBSERVATIONS:

1. The use of dots with this system does not add to the notation, but only serves to clarify what the abbreviations already indicate. The number of dots refers to the number of notes on that particular notehead.

2. When an abbreviated note is tied into a succeeding rhythm, the tie affects only the final note of the abbreviation as indicated below:

3. The use of three slashes indicates thirty-second notes in the shorthand system; however, three slashes also is the notation for a roll on percussion instruments. In this Etude, all thirty-second note abbreviations have dots to clarify the rhythms. When three slashes indicate a roll, the tr or tremolo sign is used.

INTERPRETATIONS:

The shorthand abbreviated note system works as follows:

1. One slash refers to eighth notes.

2. Two slashes refer to sixteenth notes.

3. Three slashes refer to thirty-second notes.

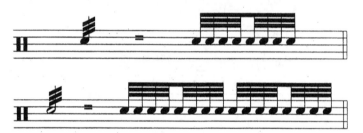

4. When a slash is used in conjunction with a flag, add the flag to the slashes to determine the abbreviation.

5. When a slash in on a dotted note, it adds the correct number of notes to the note value. If the abbreviated note has a triplet indication, the resulting rhythm is a triplet.

EL03626A

46

ETUDE #47

Etude #47 provides the perfect example for discussing the proper method of counting mixed meters. I firmly believe that if young students are taught to verbalize the rhythms they play, the mystery of counting mixed meters will not present much of a problem.

Mixed meters can simply be a grouping of 4/4, 3/ 4, and 2/4 measures. They are usually not a problem since it just requires changing the number of beats per measure. This is also true when combining groups of eighth-based time signatures, for example, 2/8, 3/8, 5/8, etc., and sixteenth-based time signatures, for example, 3/16, 4/16, 5/16, etc.

The real problems occur when these meters are combined, as in Etude #47 (i.e. 4/4, 3/16, and 5/8). The usual solution is to sing the rhythms without any formal counting system. I would like to suggest the following counting system, which I term, "rhythmic solfeggio".

1. The denominator of the time signature always receives the main count. In 3/4 time, for example, each quarter note in the measure receives one count—1,2,3. In 3/8 time, each eighth note receives one count—1,2,3,. In 3/16 time, each sixteenth note receives one count—1,2,3. The following notation shows how this looks on the staff. The speed of the eighth note is always constant throughout Etude #47.

2. The primary division of the beat is counted by the syllable <u>**an**</u>.

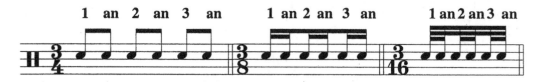

3. Dividing any main beat into three (a triplet) is counted as follows:

4. Dividing any main beat into four parts is counted as follows:

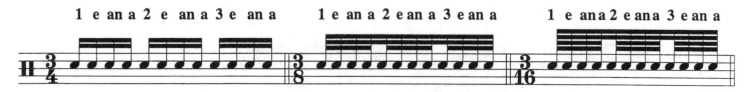

5. A simple combination of quarter-based time signatures and eighth-based time signatures would look as follows:

6. Adding sixteenth notes complicates the counting a bit further:

7. The first line of Etude #47 is counted as follows:

8. All the sixteenth-note rhythms, starting in the 7/16 measure of line 5, are counted as main beats:

9. All the triplet patterns in this piece have been explained except the sixteenth-note triplets in a quarter-based time signature. They are counted as follows (line 7, measure two):

10. Thirty-second notes in a quarter-based time signature are counted as follows:

47

This page has been left blank to facilitate page turns.

ETUDE #48

Etude #48 also functions well as a solo or recital piece because of the extreme dynamic changes, many flam and drag combinations, and rapid, soft passages—all of which require a high level of technique and control.

OBSERVATIONS:

1. I would advise learning this work by counting each eighth-note pulse at first, and then, later phrasing with four pulses per measure.

2. All the instructions relating to the flam and drag sticking in the previous Etudes also apply to Etude #48. These rules are important for a consistent sound and technical control.

3. Line 7 juxtaposes sixteenth-note triplets against thirty-second notes. Play the thirty-second notes on the quick side against the more relaxed rhythm of the triplets to effectively execute these measures.

INTERPRETATIONS:

1. I suggest using the flam tap sticking for the first measure of line 1. Use the reverse flam tap sticking for the similar passage in measure one of line 5.

2. In order for the accents in line 6 to be effective, make an effort **not** to accent the first beat of the three-note groupings.

3. Since the dynamics change so rapidly in line 9 and 10, play this entire section in the center area of the head.

EL03626A

48

Allegro con moto ♪ = 132

ETUDE #49

Etude #49 is another mixed-meter solo with all the meters having the same eighth note as the basic pulse. Similar to Etude #45, where the basic pulse is the sixteenth note, each eighth note will receive one count.

OBSERVATIONS:

1. The opening measures should be counted in the following manner:

2. As with all mixed-meter music, phrase according to the way the notes are beamed.

3. Accents will always determine how a measure will be phrased regardless of the beaming. A good example of this is in the third, fourth, and fifth measures of line 3. The third measure will now feel like a measure with two groups of 2. The fourth and fifth measures will feel like syncopation since the accents are on the off beats.

INTERPRETATIONS:

1. Although the first two measures are notated with eighth and quarter notes, in reality they will sound equal when played on the snare drum. A more accurate way of notating the first two measures is as follows:

2. Whenever a rhythm is slow enough, as with the first two measures of line 1, use one hand for all the notes in order to maintain a consistent sound.

3. The "one-hand" concept also works well for repeated off beats as in the second measure of the last line.

4. Although there is only one dynamic for the entire Etude (*f*), the section starting in line 7 has an aggressive, driving character and can be played at a louder level.

49

Allegro vivo ♩ = 138

ETUDE #50

Etude #50 acts as a grand finale, beginning with an Adagio which is actually is a series of fermatas that shows off one of the most demanding snare drum techniques—the loud roll. All tempos continually increase in speed—ending in a rapid Prestissimo.

OBSERVATIONS:

1. There are no metronome markings in this work, leaving each new tempo up to the performer's skill. The trick is to gauge each increase so there is a noticeable tempo change at each tempo marking.

2. The tempo markings of Piú allegro and Piú vivo indicate a tempo faster than the previous marking, but not as fast at the one to come.

INTERPRETATIONS:

1. The first two rolls do not have ties; the next three do—therefore, leave a slight break between measures one and two, and three and four. The three remaining measures are played as one continuous roll.

2. The last measure of line 2 has a fermata. Since this is a single stroke and not a roll, the fermata acts as a break in the tempo before line 3 begins.

3. Because of the roll and flam passages throughout the Allegro vivace, the tempo of this Etude will be dictated by the difficulty of these patterns. From the Piú vivo on, the tempos can increase at a greater rate.

50

ANTHONY J. CIRONE

Anthony J. Cirone received his bachelor of science and master of science degrees from the Juilliard School of Music where he studied with Saul Goodman, solo timpanist for the New York Philharmonic. Upon graduation, he was offered the position of percussionist with the San Francisco Symphony under Josef Krips and also an assistant professorship of music at San José State University where he has served since 1965. During his ensuing tenure at the symphony, he has performed under the baton of music directors Seiji Ozawa, Edo DeWaart, Herbert Blomstedt, and Michael Tilson Thomas and noted guest conductors such as Leonard Bernstein, Igor Stravinsky, Aaron Copland, Eugene Ormandy, Kurt Mazur, Rafael Kubelik, and James Levine.

He is currently professor of music at San José State University where he heads the percussion department and also teaches the Manuscript Preparation/Computer Engraving section of the Music Technology course. Cirone has also been on the faculty of San Francisco State University and Stanford University. His students have gone on to hold positions in major orchestras and universities around the world.

A prolific composer, he has more than sixty published titles, including textbooks, three symphonies for percussion, four sonatas, a string quartet, and five works for orchestra. He is a percussion consultant/editor for Warner Bros. Publications and is the author of *Portraits in Rhythm*, a collection of fifty studies for snare drum, used worldwide as a standard text for training percussionists in colleges and universities.

Anthony Cirone is featured in a video entitled *Concert Percussion—A Performer's Guide*, distributed by Warner Bros. Publications; he has also designed two pairs of Signature Snare Drum Sticks for Malletech Corporation; he won the *Modern Drummer* Magazine Reader's Poll for Best Classical Percussionist five years in a row; he is an active clinician; and he is involved with research and development for the Avedis Zildjian Cymbal Company.